Kissing Ban & Stolen Hearts

Bianka Minte-König

Kissing Ban & Stolen Hearts

Aus dem Deutschen
von Helena Ragg-Kirkby

Thienemann

Contents

No Kissing!

"So is Meik actually going out with you, Kiki?"

There was an unpleasant undertone of "or what?" in the question put to me by our Chief **Slug**, Gracia. What did she mean, "or what"? What was she getting at? Of course Meik was going out with me – there wasn't any 'or what' about it!

"I mean, I don't want to interfere …"

But you are interfering, I thought.

"… but if he were my boyfriend …"

"… then he'd be headed for the **loony-bin**!" I interrupted.

She gave me a poisonous look and then said, **wickedly gleeful** and drawing out her words, "Even if it's nothing to do with me …"

How true, how true!!!

"… I reckon that Meik and Mona stand a bit too close

---

slug, *hier:* Schleimschnecke;
loony-bin – Klapsmühle;
wickedly gleeful – schadenfroh, hämisch

together in the bus in the morning. You could almost think he enjoyed the way that she squeezes up to him!"

Who cared? After all, it shouldn't bother me if my favourite enemy were feeling jealous again. What else would make her spoil my new-found happiness by giving me false information? But that's what Slugs do: they **swot**, creep around, and stir up the **hotbed of rumour good and proper**! They couldn't be happy without intrigues!

"I thought you should know ..." Gracia tried once more to give me her lousy message.

Should I? No-oo! I didn't want to! I decided to shut my ears. What I don't know can't hurt me.

"They really don't have to squeeze up to one another quite so closely", Daphne – **smug** face and fellow Slug – added, taking the same line. Had the pair of them arranged this? I looked at them sharply. But either they were skilled actresses, or what they were saying was actually true.

"When I got on, they, of course, moved away from one another. They were really embarrassed, I can tell you!"

If she wanted to make me anxious, she'd **succeeded** – particularly when she added her final touch: "They've got something to hide – guaranteed!"

---

to swot – *hier:* streben;
hotbed of rumour – Gerüchteküche;
good and proper – richtig, gehörig;
smug – eingebildet, blasiert;
to succeed – Erfolg haben

Slap! Even if I didn't want to admit it, they'd **struck a blow**. And first thing in the morning, too, even before school had started. Do you really have to have your relationship thrown in your face by the Slugs when you're still half asleep? Thank God my friends Franzi and Greetje were just getting off their bus and had overheard Daphne's last sentence.

"Come on, Kiki", said Greetje, putting a friendly arm round me. "They're just jealous because you're happy with Meik."

The funny sound of her Dutch accent **dampened down** my rising anger somewhat.

Franzi, however, had **scented betrayal**. She nodded her head thoughtfully to and fro. "They're hardly going to make it up. There's no smoke without fire ... but you, of course, will know whether you can trust Meik and Mona ..."

Grr! She was only saying that because she wasn't getting anywhere with that **dozy jerk** Raffi. But that was no reason for her to **run** Meik **down** to me. Could I help having an unstable emotional life?

"I'm not running anyone down", she said, trying to **mollify** me in return for my reproach. "But as your friend, I don't want you to be temporarily blinded by love and in for a rude awakening."

---

to strike a blow – einen Schlag versetzen;
to dampen down – dämpfen; to scent – wittern;
betrayal – Verrat; dozy jerk – *hier:* Schlaftablette;
to run sb/sth down – jmdn./etwas schlecht machen;
to mollify sb – jmdn. beschwichtigen

I'd already repeatedly **gathered** that she didn't particularly like Meik, but wasn't she going a bit too far now? My blood boiled. No doubt I was turning green. I quickly had to put a stop to it.

"Thanks for your concern, but I can take care of myself!"

Was that too harsh? Franzi looked seriously **piqued**.

"Well, that surprises me, given your constant need for advice", she grumbled, presumably **alluding** to the fact that I never stopped ringing her. And with the words: "Find yourself another **agony aunt** in future!" she simply walked off towards the school without waiting for us.

Silly cow! I could surely expect my best friend not to **stab me in the back** as well, but to be on my side against the Slugs! But as always – I was no longer calm! I'd have to keep a better eye on Meik and Mona.

It wasn't just the stupid **gossip** about Meik and Mona that **wrecked** the start of school for me. The next bit of bad news was awaiting us at the school door.

"What's that all about?" I could hear Franzi crying in horror even from a distance, and Lea, the fourth member of the Pepper Dollies Club, as our clique called itself, **emitted** an astonished "Oh my God!"

---

to gather – *hier:* mitbekommen;
piqued – pikiert, gekränkt; to allude to – anspielen auf;
agony aunt – Kummerkastentante;
to stab sb in the back – jmdm. in den Rücken fallen;
gossip – Tratsch; to wreck – ruinieren;
to emit – ausstoßen

Greetje and I stared in irritation at the canary-yellow notice that was demanding attention on the main door to the school. Proving its official status **by virtue of** its school stamp and the signature of the new headmistress, Frau Biedermann, it made an unbelievable statement. My **row** with Franzi was forgotten just like that.

"Do you read what I read?" asked Franzi, fluttering her eyelashes, evidently attempting to chase away a supposed mirage. **In vain**. The notice was no **tissue of fantasy** but bitter reality.

I swallowed, for my eyes almost dropped out of my head when I read the long list of ***Addenda*** *to the School Rules*. I had, it's true, had a feeling since Friday that we were in for something along these lines. Then our class teacher and acting headmaster, Dr. Wolf, had introduced the new Head to us in the hall. Frau Biedermann – our **school governors'** response to the Pisa Study. The desire for change that had been evident in her **inaugural** speech had been anything other than wishy-washy, and I had already had the feeling then that we were going to have to be prepared for trouble under her regime. But nobody could ever have guessed that she would **get stuck in** so quickly, practically overnight! I sighed.

---

by virtue of – aufgrund; row – *hier:* Streit;
in vain – vergeblich; tissue of fantasy – Hirngespinst;
addendum, addenda (pl) – Zusatz;
school governor – *hier:* Stiftungsrat; inaugural – Antritts-;
to get stuck in – loslegen

Bans and **punishments**! Nothing but punishments and bans. The entire long list read like an **instruction manual** for the so-called **poisonous pedagogy** that children were **tortured** with in the eighteenth century. We'd done an interesting project on it last year for the school's anniversary. "School in the olden days." Wow, was I ever glad that I was alive now and not then. But now it appeared that the past was catching up with us!

Bans on smoking, mobiles and chewing gum. Bans on **swearing** and **insults**, on physical fights and **scrapping**. Bans on spitting and copying from one another. Punishments for being late, for leaving the school **premises**, for dropping litter in school or in the playground. Bans on provocative clothing and – surely I wasn't seeing properly – a ban on sexual acts on the school premises!

"Did I read that rightly?" I shook my head **in disbelief**.

"What does that mean? Sexual acts?" asked Greetje, who still struggled a bit to read German texts.

"Well, what do you think?" cried Lea. "Kissing!"

"Tell me that's not true! Has our new headmistress spent too long in the sun?" I just didn't get it.

"You think she's got **sunstroke**?"

---

ban – Verbot; punishment – Bestrafung;
instruction manual – Gebrauchsanleitung;
poisonous pedagogy – *hier:* Schwarze Pädagogik;
to torture – foltern; to swear – fluchen;
insult – Beleidigung; scrapping – *hier:* Rangelei;
premises (pl) – Gelände; in disbelief – ungläubig;
sunstroke – Sonnenstich

Sunstroke would at least be a plausible explanation for such an abnormal action. A normal, healthy human mind just couldn't come up with something like this!

"Her brain must have **evaporated** in the sauna", said Franzi without respect. "Kissing banned on the school premises!" She tapped her head. "I reckon she's **nuts**!"

And Greetje added, "She's not right up there."

After what I'd read, I had no choice but to agree entirely.

"She's really banned kissing on the entire school premises?" I asked **all the same**, just to make sure. It could be that I'd misunderstood some part of the notice. But when my friends all nodded it was obvious that nobody had got the date wrong and was playing an April Fool joke on us.

Some unfortunate impulse had caused our new headmistress to make completely **lunatic** changes to the school rules – and thereby to **encroach** massively **on** our human rights. As the daughter of an **MP**, there's no way I could **approve of** this. And, evidently, nor could my fellow pupils.

At any rate, a large crowd of angry people had gathered by the door, and expressions of **annoyance** were growing from within the mass.

---

to evaporate – verdampfen; to be nuts – verrückt sein;
all the same – trotzdem; lunatic – blödsinnig;
to encroach on – eingreifen in; MP = member of parliament – MdB = Mitglied des Bundestages;
to approve of – zustimmen; at any rate – jedenfalls;
annoyance – Verärgerung

"Who I kiss and when I kiss them," our class caveman Fabian was just yelling, "is nobody's business but my own!" And giving me an **insinuating** look, he called, "Isn't that right, Kiki? It's none of the school's business!"

I was still feeling angry with him for showing me up just because he didn't want to understand that I had zero interest in him, when a voice right behind me called, "I agree!"

At that moment I felt someone grab my arm. Someone pulled me to him and pressed a passionate kiss on my lips in front of the gathered crowd. Meik!

But before I could come to my senses the door suddenly flew open and the new headmistress filled the door-frame with all the power of her position.

"Caught you!" she said gleefully, pointing to Meik and me. You could tell from her voice that she was positively rubbing her hands **inwardly**.

I **disentangled myself from** Meik's arms as quickly as possible and bowed my head, playing the **penitent** little **sinner**. But Fabian and his gang of Gorillas, who'd **presumably** gone mad, immediately undertook a spontaneous protest action, and grabbed the first females they could get hold of before beginning a wild, demonstrative **snog**-fest. Of course the girls immediately started squealing in panic and tried to get away. How-

---

insinuating – *hier:* anzüglich; inward – innerlich;
to disentangle oneself from – sich befreien von/aus;
penitent – reuig; sinner – Sünder/in;
presumable – vermutlich; to snog – knutschen

ever **keen** they might have been to defend the freedom of kissing, having to be kissed by the Gorillas of all people is not something that could be expected of any girl! This would **amount to** giving a blank cheque to all our **would-be** macho-men and would mean choosing to **bin** all the achievements of the Women's Movement.

"Off to the Head's office with you!" commanded the authoritative voice of Frau Biedermann.

But I couldn't take my eyes off the **commotion** at the bottom of the school steps.

"You get your hands off me!" Lea was just screaming as she pushed Fabian away from her with all her **might**. He fell backwards, pulling a number of curious onlookers to the ground with him. Greetje was just drawing back her arm to give Sebastian a **clout**. However, he ducked, and so her slap in the face landed mistakenly in precisely the sort of face you'd like to slap: that of Gracia, Chief Slug. Damn you! I grinned, full of schadenfreude. After all the trouble she'd given me that morning, I really wasn't capable of feeling much **sympathy**.

Gracia squealed hysterically, held her cheek and howled, "I'm telling my mother, she's **chairwoman** of the **PTA**. You'll get **expelled**!"

---

to be keen (on) – erpicht sein (auf);
to amount to – hinauslaufen auf; would-be – Möchtegern;
to bin – wegwerfen; commotion – Aufruhr;
might – Macht, Kraft; clout – *hier:* Ohrfeige;
sympathy – Mitleid; chairwoman – Vorsitzende;
PTA = Parent Teacher Association – Elternrat;
to expel – hinauswerfen

I felt a hand grab my shoulder. "Off you go – didn't you hear? To the Head's office with you!"

I was about to submit to the **inexorable** command when I spotted Franzi in the crowd.

I couldn't believe it! I poked Meik in the ribs and pointed to them. We both had to laugh out loud.

Franzi had evidently **seized** the moment, for she was intimately embracing a boy who was at least a head shorter than her, and she was snogging him **with abandon**. Raffi! She'd done it at last! She'd been trying to get off with him for months, and now she'd **boldly** seized the opportunity. Well, now she'd see my being in love through different eyes and with more understanding!

Giggling, we detached ourselves from the scene that was building up, and let Frau Biedermann **usher** us in the direction of her **study**.

Neither of us expected a serious punishment. After all, our **esteemed** Frau Headmistress must have seen what her orders had **sparked off**. And if she had any hint of intelligence, she'd immediately call it all off. That's what we thought. It was logical. Wasn't it?

No, it wasn't, however, for pupil logic and teacher logic don't necessarily lead to the same conclusions. She, at any rate, didn't **remotely** think of cancelling anything, and had only one thing on her mind: making

---

inexorable – unerbittlich; to seize – ergreifen, nutzen;
with abandon – leidenschaftlich; bold – mutig;
to giggle – kichern; to usher – führen; study – *hier:* Büro;
esteemed – geschätzt; to spark off – auslösen;
remotely – im Entferntesten

an example out of Meik and me that would scare all the other pupils off breaking the kissing ban or any other part of the school rules.

She was, therefore, **impervious to** all our arguments, and growled that we were to spend a week doing "community" work, which meant – how mega-embarrassing – **sweeping** the **playground** and removing old chewing gum from the desks. The very thought of it was enough to make you **puke**. Just imagine it: Fabian plucking a **chunky lump** of chewing gum out of his mouth, grinning stupidly at you and gleefully sticking it under the desk. Saying **patronisingly** as he did so, "To give you something to do." Grrr!

Pretty fed up, Meik and I returned to our classrooms. Lessons had started meanwhile, and the **incipient** revolt had evidently somehow been brought under control by the teachers.

"Do you reckon that's it?" I asked. "Do you think the others will accept the kissing ban?"

Meik shook his head. "I don't imagine so. Most of the other measures need to be discussed, too. They cancel out all the freedoms that the school council **reps** have struggled to force through in recent years. Quite apart from such ridiculous things as the ban on snogging!"

"What do you think she means by provocative clothing?" I asked.

---

impervious to – unzugänglich für; to sweep – kehren; playground – *hier:* Schulhof; to puke – sich übergeben; chunky – fett; lump – Klumpen; patronising – gönnerhaft; incipient – beginnend; rep = representative – Vertreter

Meik grinned as he looked at my T-shirt with its small **bumps** and which bore the **legend** *Sex Bomb.*

Then he pointed his index finger at my **belly button** which was **cheekily** peeping out and said with a wink, tickling my stomach as he did so, "That there, for instance!"

I giggled.

"Frau Biedermann's arranged a school assembly. Presumably to justify her measures", said Meik. "There'll no doubt be **heaps of** protests against this nonsense. For me, at any rate, it's completely unacceptable." He grinned at me cheekily. "Well, do you **fancy** rebelling a bit?" And with these words he pulled me into his arms again and kissed me **defiantly**.

"So you won't learn!" thundered a powerful voice behind us. Frau Biedermann! Didn't she have anything better to do than creep around school corridors lying in wait for pupils in love? Wolfie, my class teacher, was standing next to her.

"You see, Herr Dr. Wolf," said the headmistress, her voice **oozing** satisfaction, "iron discipline is the only think that will work here. The kind of indulgence that you have in mind will achieve nothing. The Pisa Study on the achievement levels of our pupils in comparison to the rest of Europe has shocked us all. But is any-

---

bump – *hier:* Wölbung; legend – Aufschrift;
belly button – Bauchnabel; cheeky – frech;
heaps of – Massen von;
to fancy sb/sth – jmdn./etwas gern mögen;
defiant – herausfordernd; to ooze – *hier:* strotzen vor

thing actually being done about the embarrassingly poor standing of German schoolchildren? No! Hanging around, flirting, video and computer games … their heads are filled with nothing but **junk**. Let me tell you, this is going to become a **beacon** school. Pupils will study here in future without distractions. Yes indeed! Until our pupils are the best in Europe again. And until then, all my rules will remain in place. All of them!"

She turned to us again.

"Two weeks of sweeping the playground instead of one! And if I catch you engaged in sexual acts again, you will get a **black mark** on your **reports**! Now off you go to your classrooms!"

Before I knew where I was, Wolfie had grabbed my hand and was pulling me into the corridor which led to my classroom.

"Come on," he hissed. "And **for goodness' sake**, keep your mouth shut."

Once we'd got round the corner and out of sight, he stopped and let go of my hand. He was out of breath and seemed stressed. "She's a very intelligent woman. A very high **achiever**. She's got a legendary reputation when it comes to **licking** schools **into shape**. The school governors sent her in to turn us into a beacon school."

---

junk – Müll; beacon – *hier:* Vorzeige-;
black mark – *hier:* Eintrag; report – *hier:* Zeugnis;
for goodness' sake – um Himmels willen;
achiever – Überflieger;
to lick sth into shape – etwas auf Vordermann bringen

He **gasped for breath**, then added, in a **plea** for understanding: "We'll be a model school and we'll get millions in **subsidies**. Everyone will benefit. We'll be able to buy computers, video cameras, new lab equipment for Chemistry and Physics ..."

Before he could rave on any more, I stopped him with a defiant interruption. "And for that we have to sell our freedom! Great! I wouldn't have expected that from you, Herr Wolf."

He looked kind of unhappily at me with his puppy-dog eyes, and his slightly greying **moustache** trembled. "I ... um ... we just have to wait ... she's only just started. Everything can always be discussed, no doubt with her, too ..."

I reckon he was wrong there.

On the way to my seat I passed Mona's desk.

"Was it awful?" she asked inquisitively.

I **shrugged my shoulders**. Seeing her immediately reminded me of Gracia's **suspicions**. I gave her a mistrustful look.

Since the fashion show we'd **buried the hatchet**, but had we really buried it deeply enough? Had a little shared revenge campaign against a lousy caveman really been sufficient to create a **lasting** friendship between us?

---

to gasp for breath – nach Luft schnappen;
plea – Bitte; subsidy – Zuschuss; moustache – Schnurrbart;
to shrug one's shoulders – die Schultern zucken;
suspicion – Verdacht;
to bury the hatchet – das Kriegsbeil begraben;
lasting – dauerhaft

Wasn't she too good-looking for any boy to be able to resist her? Especially when the **jam-packed** bus in the morning meant that she was constantly pressing up against him? A boy would have to be **gay** not to be turned on by that kind of thing, well-known for making people fall in love! Then I remembered the passionate kisses just now, and shrugged my shoulders again. So what! The sweet way Meik had kissed me made one thing clear: that there was only one person he loved, namely me!

Wolfie's lesson, normally pretty pleasant and peaceful, was suffering today from his evident **lack of** concentration. And ours. I normally found Geography as dry as dust anyway and today in particular, the subject did nothing at all for me. The others presumably felt the same. Fabian put his hand up. However, when Wolfie picked on him, he didn't give an answer to the question **at hand** on the geo-formation of the Swabian Alb, but asked, "Herr Wolf, couldn't we have a spontaneous **form period** instead? I think the whole class feels a bit in need of advice at the moment."

Wolfie turned red because he, of course, immediately knew what Fabian was alluding to. The kissing ban. Everyone wanted to know how a headmistress could come up with the idea of **issuing** such a provocative rule.

---

jam-packed – gestopft voll; gay – schwul;
lack of – Mangel an; at hand – *hier:* gestellt;
form period – Klassenlehrerstunde; to issue – *hier:* erlassen

Wolfie turned away under our expectant glances. He was one of those really nice teachers who never in fact had any trouble from pupils. But he was also a man of principles and believed that school ought to be the most important thing in a pupil's life. He was very **cross** with me, for instance, when I **skived off** lessons so that I could take part in a modelling competition. Even though my mother excused me, he entered my name in the register for unauthorised absence. In that way he was mega old-fashioned.

So far as love between the pupils **was concerned**, he was evidently equally old-fashioned. For what he had to say about the kissing ban sounded anything but hopeful for us. Of course a good deal of **muttering** started up in the rows when he tried to win us over to the measures.

"It can't be that bad, doing without exchanging such intimate **caresses** during school hours," he said in all seriousness. "That kind of thing really doesn't belong in public. I also believe that this **permissiveness** has started to be taken too far."

Almost everyone booed at these words. Only the Slugs – Gracia, Daphne and Lydia clapped. Nobody would choose to kiss them anyway! I stared at the **stuck-up** cows angrily, but couldn't help grinning.

---

cross – sauer; to skive off – schwänzen;
so far as … is concerned – was … betrifft; to mutter – murren;
caress – Zärtlichkeit; permissiveness – Freizügigkeit;
stuck-up – eingebildet

Gracia's **cheek** still bore the faint imprint of Greetje's right hand, that had **whacked** her by mistake.

Mona put her hand up. "Herr Wolf, don't you also think that this measure represents an **undue** interference in the pupils' intimate sphere?"

"In the … what?" asked Sebastian, his mouth dropping open with surprise.

Well, didn't Mona ever have an astonishing vocabulary!

"The school can't regulate every single expression of life in its pupils," she said. "They can't forbid us to go to the **loo** if we need to …"

"That's different," replied Wolfie. "Or are you trying to say that kissing is the same as **relieving oneself**?"

He shouldn't have said that.

The Gorillas positively laughed themselves under their desks.

And they had the least reason to laugh. If flirting took on the character of relieving oneself for any of us, it would be for these sex-mad guys. They couldn't live without being **on the pull**!

I exchanged eloquent but amused looks with my friends from the Pepper Dollies. Wolfie had unquestionably scored a classic own goal. Oh, he was so awkward and out of touch sometimes! That joke would have to go into the next yearbook. I made myself a note.

---

cheek – Wange; to whack – schlagen; undue – unzulässig;
loo – Klo; to relieve oneself – sich erleichtern;
to be on the pull – auf Männer-/Frauenfang sein

Wolfie's red face had turned **a couple of shades** darker. How lovely that inner **turmoil** sometimes expressed itself for teachers in such an embarrassing way as it did for us pupils.

I always wanted the ground to swallow me up in such situations. Since I could imagine that Wolfie felt the same at that moment, I **gave in** to the pity that spontaneously sprang up inside me and tried to help him out of his **fix**.

"Herr Wolf, how do the other teachers see these measures?" I asked, in an attempt to steer him away from the embarrassing topic.

Wolfie shrugged his shoulders and didn't speak.

"The teachers are guaranteed to be right behind them ..." Fabian muttered to the class.

"I'm not so sure about that," cried Franzi, and Greetje protested, "My father isn't, no way would he join in with that kind of thing!"

But Mona added sceptically, "They don't have any choice even if they want to ... Frau Biedermann is kind of like their superior. If that's what she wants to do, the teachers have to go along with it, or else they might as well start **submitting** their **resignation applications**!"

"Just because it's a private school?" I asked.

Gracia gave me a **filthy** look. "Yes, precisely because

---

a couple of – einige;
shade – Schattierung; turmoil – Aufruhr;
to give in – nachgeben; fix – Klemme, Patsche;
to submit one's resignation application – seine Kündigung einreichen; filthy – *hier:* giftig

of that. My mother said Frau Biedermann would bring a bit of order to this school at long last, so that German pupils can get the top spots in Europe again. And my mother's on the PTA."

That was the second time I'd heard this. My mother's on the PTA! Huh! And, angry about this stuck-up cow, I thought, 'My father's an MP, and he'll tell your mother and Frau Biedermann where they can get off with their trampling on our democratic rights! Private school or no private school!'

Wolfie gave up. Five minutes before the bell he gathered up his things and murmured, "Read page 141 until break-time and write a summary of it for tomorrow." And then he hastened out of the classroom.

So much for relieving oneself: had all the stress gone straight to his **bladder**, perhaps?

Needless to say, nobody read the **aforementioned** pages. On the contrary, a heated discussion broke out between the Slugs and the rest of the class about the legitimacy of the prescribed ban on snogging – which was, however, interrupted by the bell.

Like wild things, all the pupils immediately rushed to the hall, which was soon jam-packed.

A slim boy of medium height whom I'd already noticed several times in the playground **on account of** his freaky dreadlocks was standing at the **lectern**. Next to

---

bladder – Blase; aforementioned – zuvor erwähnt;
on account of – wegen; lectern – Rednerpult

him was Mariam from Meik's class. Evidently, the **student heads**. Meik, Fabian and other year reps were on stage, too.

"We'll sort it out," the boy with the dreadlocks was just saying. "We're still waiting for our new headmistress, Frau Biedermann, and the co-ordinators and **staff**-pupil **liaison** teachers."

As he spoke, a little group of teachers made their way onto the stage. My favourite teacher van Gogh, Greetje's father who took us for Art, was among them. He was seriously popular among the students and for that reason was also on the staff-pupil liaison **body**. He went straight to the microphone.

"Thanks very much, Bastian," he said to the student head and bent over the microphone. Like Bastian, he tried to calm the angry pupils, but had no more success than the **former**.

Suddenly, however, a silence fell which spread from the hall entrance over the rows of chairs at the back and right up to the stage at the front. Like a **bow-wave**, it accompanied the self-assured figure of our headmistress, who made her way through the crowd with unshakeable calm. This in-your-face self-confidence knocked me over. As she walked – nay, **strode** – past me, it simply took my breath away, and my **resounding**, re-

---

student heads – Schulsprecher; staff – *hier:* Lehrerschaft;
liaison – Verbindung; body – Körperschaft, Gremium;
the former – der Erstere; bow-wave – Bugwelle;
to stride – schreiten; resounding – *hier:* durchdringend

bellious boo became a **croaky** little baa which remained stuck to my **vocal cords**. How embarrassing. Especially when I, a tried-and-tested election campaigner, could shout practically anyone down.

Frau Biedermann mounted the stage and walked to the lectern, where she did unto van Gogh what he had done unto Bastian. She pushed him aside and took possession of the sole microphone.

"Now she's in charge," Lea rightly observed, and Franzi added, "Watch out! The Empire Strikes Back!"

I was standing with the Pepper Dollies in the canteen, queueing for the salad buffet. The whole atmosphere was **irritable**. Our headmistress may have **quashed** the open **uprising** with her – admittedly – brilliant speech, but the general sense of anger persisted, **pervading** everything. The boy in front of me banged the salad servers into the bowl so violently that the dressing splashed right onto the tablecloth. Of course I immediately jumped backwards so as not to mess up my clothes. In the process I **trod** entirely accidentally on the **sandaled** toes of our **RE** teacher, Birkenstock. Or to put it more precisely, on his unprotected toes. He grimaced with pain and I quickly took a step forwards. Without looking, of course, as I had turned my head to Birken-

---

croaky – heiser; vocal cords – Stimmbänder;
to quash – niederschlagen; irritable – gereizt;
uprising – Aufruhr; to pervade – durchdringen;
to tread – treten; sandaled – in Sandalen;
RE = Religious Education – Religionslehre

stock to apologise for my **mishap**. However, I hadn't managed to take so much as a deep breath when a hysterical voice screeched behind me, "It wasn't me! Kiki pushed me!"

I whirled round and could already see out of the corner of my eye that Gracia was trying to justify herself to a boy who was **spattered** from head to toe in salad and dressing. Whoops, was I some kind of spiritist medium who could **conjure up** poltergeist phenomena? Why else did plates, ice-cream dishes and other **china** develop a mind of their own more often than average in my presence?

It wasn't me, flashed through my mind. This time it definitely wasn't me. Why did she have to stand in such a stupid way that a little **nudge** turned a tiny mishap into the end of the world. Despite being firmly convinced of my innocence, I fled all the same, and squeezed into the queue behind Mona.

Ha, she wasn't the only one who could squeeze up to someone!

Mona gave me a friendly grin and nodded her head towards the teachers' table. "It seems to be kicking off," she said.

Where a refined atmosphere normally **prevailed** at their table, an explosion **was** evidently **imminent**. Van

---

mishap – Missgeschick; spattered – bespritzt;
to conjure up – heraufbeschwören; china – *hier:* Geschirr;
nudge – Schubs; to prevail – vorherrschen;
to be imminent – nahe bevorstehen

Gogh, at any rate, seemed to be **at** serious **loggerheads with** Wolfie, whose face was bright red again. And Logel, our Maths teacher, was just about to **chuck** a forkful of spaghetti – fork included – at our strict English teacher Frau Ingrimm. At any rate, he'd just sprung up in anger, and only Birkenstock's **placatory efforts** had convinced him to sit down again.

I was relieved to see Birkenstock back in action. My treading on his foot couldn't have hurt him that much. I'd apologise to him before the next RE lesson.

"So, have you got a plan?" asked Mona **without further ado**.

Hmm. Did we have a plan? We certainly did, but we hadn't had a chance to discuss anything specific. Should I **pump** her a bit? After all, she wasn't entirely uncreative. Maybe she had some exciting idea that we could use against our new headmistress. But before we could exchange brainwaves, the queue had moved along so much that we had to sort out our food.

I reached for the salad servers and **aimlessly heaped** lettuce, tomatoes and slices of **cucumber** onto my plate, shovelled croutons on top, and poured dressing over the lot.

Then I picked my way **precariously** across to the table where Franzi and the other Pepper Dollies had

---

to be at loggerheads with sb – sich mit jmdm. in den Haaren liegen; to chuck – schmeißen; placatory – besänftigend; effort – Bemühung; without further ado – ohne Umschweife; to pump sb – jmdn. ausquetschen; aimless – ziellos; to heap – häufen; cucumber – Gurke; precarious – unsicher

saved me a place. Mona followed me, took a chair from the next table and sat down with us.

I could tell by looking at Franzi that it didn't in fact suit her, but she didn't say anything. Ever since Mona had turned down her invitation to join the Pepper Dollies, Franzi had completely had it with her, and she wasn't all that welcome in our group.

"What was all that about just now with Gracia?" Lea asked with a giggle. "Were you involved, Kiki?"

Greetje laughed and said, "The guy looked like a real Arcimboldo."

"Like what?" I asked, irritated.

"You know, like a picture by that painter, the one with all the vegetable faces. The man with the cucumber for a nose and stuff ..."

I vaguely remembered her father showing us a picture like that in an Art lesson. It had indeed been composed of nothing but fruit and veg. It looked funny, and there was in fact a certain similarity between this picture and Gracia's victim. Even though the boy only had a cucumber slice for a nose rather than an entire cucumber. I grinned inwardly at the comparison, but shook my head. "I didn't do anything ..."

Greetje looked disbelieving.

"No-o, honestly, I didn't ... I mean ... I might just have happened to bump into her elbow ... because ... I mean ... I trod ... by mistake, of course ... I trod on Birkenstock's toes ... and ... well ... I don't know ... it just happened." I stared at the grinning faces of my friends. "Even though you obviously don't believe a word I'm saying: it wasn't me this time!"

Franzi laughed and said **mock-sceptically**, "Who knows. Anyone who throws ice-cream dishes around isn't going to stop at salad plates."

I was cross. Did she really have to **blab** all my secrets? It was nothing to do with anyone else that I'd **tipped** a bowl of ice-cream into Meik's lap on our first date.

"Too right!" I said threateningly. "So you'd better watch out!"

And I accompanied my words with a raised salad plate.

She threw her arms up in the air defensively and **begged** in mock panic: "No, no! **Spare** me, please! Remember that physical fights are forbidden, or do you want to turn sweeping the playground into a permanent job?"

Resignedly, I put my plate back on the table. "Okay! But your luck really was in."

We'd just started eating when the guy with the dreadlocks came over to our table and deposited a couple of leaflets about the school party.

"Hi, Mona!" he said **casually** in passing, and I wondered how on earth the pair of them knew one another.

When he was already well and truly at the next table, I stole an envious glance at Mona. Why on earth did every boy seem to be mad about her? What did she have that I hadn't got? I walked like a model and wore trendy

---

mock-sceptical – gespielt skeptisch; to blab – ausplaudern;
to tip – kippen; to beg – flehen; to spare – verschonen;
resigned – resigniert; casual – locker

clothes, yet all the boys just **gawped** at her. It was so irritating!

My inner **governess** immediately demanded a word. *Cool down! Why all the jealousy?,* she whispered down my ear. ***At the end of the day****, you've got Meik. Doesn't that count for anything?*

I had to smile to myself. Of course that counted for something – **with knobs on**! To be precise, it was the only thing that counted!

I **cast a** loving **glance** at Year Nine's table, where Meik was sitting with his mates. He caught the glance, made his lips into a kiss shape and blew a **smacker** over to me. I looked around to make sure nobody had seen it. It could well be that such things were a punishable **offence** nowadays, and I really didn't want to spend three weeks pulling off chewing gum and sweeping the playground!

---

to gawp – gaffen; governess – Gouvernante;
at the end of the day – schließlich; with knobs on – allerdings;
to cast a glance – einen Blick werfen; smacker – Schmatzer;
offence – Vergehen

We have to come up with a plan

I was on my way home. My brother was **traipsing** next to me; he was in Year Five and generally known as The Joker – or just Joker for short – in our family. Because of his sunny **disposition**, of course. He seemed to have lost it today, however, as he looked as if he were about to burst into tears at any moment.

Music blared from an open window. *I will survive!*

I **hummed** along, but was **by no means** so sure that I'd survive what was awaiting me at school. Two weeks of sweeping the playground!!!

Suddenly my brother burst out, "She wants us to wear short trousers! I'd rather kill myself than wear such a stupid school uniform!"

A couple of angry tears did in fact roll down his pale cheeks.

"I'm not going to be the town clown!"

I looked down at him. A skinny boy in outsized

---

to traipse – latschen; disposition – Veranlagung, Gemüt;
to hum – summen; by no means – ganz und gar nicht

skater jeans with **hems** that he trod on with every step. The edges of the **seams** were correspondingly trendy and **frayed**. His **hooded** sweatshirt with some skater logo flapped around his body. He looked like all his friends did.

Why bother with a school uniform, I thought, the boys have had one for ages.

"Short trousers!" My brother's voice sounded as if he'd been forced to eat a plate of **tripe.**

"And she wants us to wear **demure** skirts and blazers so that we don't show off our belly buttons so provocatively," I sighed. He wasn't the only one suffering the hard knocks of fate.

"But I can't be seen in public in short trousers! Am I a little kid or what?"

"She said it would **increase** the pupils' sense of **belonging**. And that it made a point to the outside world. And that school uniforms were worn right across Europe: in Italy, France, England ..."

"With short trousers?"

"Presumably. She'll have seen it somewhere. All the same, I can't imagine it. Just imagine Raffi with those stick-insect legs of his in short trousers!"

My brother was silent. It was evidently clear to him that his legs wouldn't look any better in short trousers.

So we walked along silently for a while, each of us thinking our own thoughts.

---

hem – *hier:* Hosenbein; seam – Saum; frayed – ausgefranst; hooded – mit Kapuze; tripe – Kutteln; demure – *hier:* züchtig; to increase – erhöhen; belonging – *hier:* Zusammengehörigkeit

To be honest, I found it difficult to **digest** the morning's events. First of all these **perfidious** changes to the school rules including the kissing ban, then the assembly, and finally that – I had to admit it – mega-clever speech by our new headmistress.

Instead of **dealing with** the kissing ban, she'd given a speech about how badly we'd done in the Pisa Study, and challenged us to **restore** our honour. That in itself got her a round of applause. It died off a bit when she started talking about the team effort that was needed to improve our performance. She finally demanded that we join **extra-curricular** clubs, and that **tutorial** programmes be set up in which the older pupils were to help the younger ones with reading and Maths. In itself, a good idea.

However, she **diverged** completely **from** the kissing ban by dropping a further bombshell. With great tactical skill, she announced the immediately imminent introduction of a school uniform.

Nobody could ever have remembered the entire list of changes she was proposing, but this one was **seared on** every brain. Particularly because it didn't just apply to the older pupils but to the **titches**, too.

A **howl** went through the entire assembly.

However, as she left the hall with a perfectly **erect**

---

to digest – verdauen; perfidious – hinterhältig;
to deal with – *hier:* eingehen auf; to restore – wiederherstellen;
extra-curricular – außerschulisch; tutorial – Nachhilfe-;
to diverge from – ablenken von; to be seared on – eingebrannt sein in; titch – Knirps; howl – Aufheulen

posture and an expression accustomed to victory, we could all believe that she'd be carrying through all the measures she'd announced.

Meik wouldn't be able to tickle my belly button again. Poo!

"And what about the kissing ban?" My brother took up what was for me that most important topic of the day. "I saw her catch you and Meik. What kind of punishment did she **lumber** you **with**?"

I told him.

"She's foul," said Joker resignedly. "Mega-foul!"

When I opened the front door, Snuffles jumped up at me, yapping and **wagging** her tail. It had been a long day for her, too, and she needed to go out as quickly as possible.

"Go on," I said. "**Do a wee** before your bladder bursts!" And turning to Joker I asked, "Do you want to go with her?"

But he was already on his way to watch *Das Jugendgericht* on television. That female judge had an unusually relaxing effect on the mental state of stressed-out schoolchildren. And the **public prosecutor** even more so. Once he really got to work ... He did, it's true, bear a distant similarity to Frau Biedermann. Both pretty **grumpy**!

---

erect posture – aufrechte Haltung;
to lumber sb with sth – *hier:* jmdm. etwas aufbrummen;
to wag – *hier:* wedeln; to do a wee – pinkeln;
public prosecutor – Staatsanwalt; grumpy – mürrisch, verbiestert

I grabbed Snuffles and took her round the block. My dog pulled me along, full of energy, and I **pondered** about how we could trick our new headmistress.

The firmness with which she'd controlled the mob at the assembly did **compel** my respect. Her manner was something quite new to us. She didn't seem like a teacher but like the manager of a big industrial firm. And that's how she seemed to view her job, too. But all the same, I had the impression that something was wrong somewhere. She put on a good solo performance, but what a school really demanded was teamwork.

The co-ordinators and staff-pupil liaison teachers had all **hovered around** looking rather uncomfortable at this turn of events, and were **bound to** feel as if they'd been **bypassed**. Did that ever **smack of** problems! No doubt we'd be able to get a couple of teachers onto our side.

I pulled Snuffles away from a dog that she was just about to snap at, and sighed.

Whatever, our new headmistress was certainly a powerful woman. We could count on that. She was capable of doing absolutely everything she'd announced.

Back at home, I made a vanilla tea, threw myself in front of the TV, and switched a music channel on. Pink was just starting the party and I hummed along. I just didn't

---

to ponder – nachdenken; to compel – *hier:* abnötigen;
to hover around – herumstehen; to be bound to – müssen;
to be bypassed – übergangen werden;
to smack of – riechen nach

get why the teachers had to run down television in our media studies lessons. What was wrong with a bit of escaping from reality? It was mega-relaxing not to have to think about your everyday worries for once. When Jeanette Biedermann appeared, however, she immediately reminded me of our headmistress, and all my relaxation **vanished** just like that. I reached for the phone and rang Franzi.

She was always the best **tonic** at depressive moments. Today, however, she seemed to **be at sixes and sevens** as well, because she took forever to come to the phone, and then she didn't listen to me properly.

"So what's the matter with you?" I finally asked her, irritated. "What's on your mind?"

But at the very moment I asked the question, I knew the answer for myself. Oh, was I ever **insensitive**! Of course she was thinking about Raffi, whom she'd kissed for the first time today.

"Forgive me, please forgive me! What a lousy friend I am! And I even saw it with my own eyes!" I **pleaded**.

I almost fell over myself to be **sympathetic** just in order to **rectify** my mistake and to **erase** the impression that I wasn't really interested in my best friend's fate.

To be honest, I couldn't remotely imagine that they were a good match, but at the end of the day, it wasn't

---

to vanish – verschwinden; tonic – *hier:* Aufmunterung;
to be at sixes and sevens – durcheinander sein;
insensitive – unsensibel; to plead – bitten;
sympathetic – mitfühlend; to rectify – wieder gutmachen;
to erase – *hier:* ausmerzen

my job to interfere. **Poking my nose into** Franzi's love-life in the way she poked her nose into mine really wasn't my thing. So I congratulated her. "Congratulations! It's finally worked out with Raffi!" And I dutifully followed it up with the obligatory question: "So, what was it like? What kind of kisser is he?"

A **torrent** of words poured into my ear. It was just as if Franzi had been waiting to blow every detail of her **wondrous** happiness down someone's **auditory canal**.

Okay, okay, she was in credit with me, but when after ten minutes I was hearing for the hundred-and-thirtieth – or thereabouts – time about what a sensitive kisser Raffi was and that he was simply the most snoggable and sweetest boy in our entire school, then I felt that she'd used up all her credit **at one fell swoop**.

"Franzi," I said, brutally interrupting her **besotted** whisperings, "it's **fab** that you and Raffi have got together. But it's undoubtedly the only good thing our new headmistress has brought about. Everything else is absolutely catastrophic. Get it? All these new rules are a complete catastrophe."

"True," agreed Franzi without, however, immediately coming up with a creative idea to solve the problem as she normally did.

She's in love, I thought frustratedly. She really can't see what's going on around her.

---

to poke one's nose into sth – seine Nase in etwas stecken;
torrent – Schwall; wondrous – wundersam;
auditory canal – Gehörgang; at one fell swoop – auf einen Schlag;
besotted – *hier:* verliebt; fab = fabulous – fantastisch

Horrors! My best **ally** in the battle against the rigours of fate and the evils of the world was out of the fight and lying on **fluffy Cloud Nine**. Poo! So was I now supposed to sort this mess out on my own? Oh no-oo!

I tried a renewed **appeal** to her rational mind. "We have to do something. We can't let ourselves be trampled on by such an authoritarian person!"

"True," she repeated, and it didn't sound a single scrap more engaged.

So I had to bring out the big guns.

"Hey, come off your cloud," I grumbled at her. "There's more than a flirtation **at stake** here: it's a question of surviving in that school! If we don't do something, it's the first and last time you'll ever kiss Raffi at school!"

That worked. The seriousness of the situation was now clear to her, too.

"You're right." She finally found her way back to grey reality. "We'll have to discuss the whole thing with all the Pepper Dollies. I'll text Lea and you text Greetje."

Sorted! I hung up.

Just at the right moment, as Mum pushed my bedroom door open with her elbow and came in **juggling** two plates of cream cakes.

"Hello, Kiki," she said cheerfully, **full of beans** again. "Have you got a sip of tea left for me?"

---

ally – Verbündete/r; fluffy – flauschig;
Cloud Nine – Wolke sieben; appeal – Appell;
to be at stake – auf dem Spiel stehen; to juggle – jonglieren;
full of beans – gut gelaunt

Of course I had. After all, we always had the same ritual on Mondays. It was the day on which she came home from the advertising agency before bedtime for once, and the late afternoon tea ritual was one of its essential parts. Since my brother preferred **malt** beer and Dragon Ball, it was always a little girly **gossip** session.

Mum threw herself down on my Pop Sofa, gratefully took the full cup of tea I offered her, stirred her sugar stick around in it for a while, lost in thought, and then said after the first appreciative sip, "So how was school? Is the new headmistress nice?"

I almost **choked** on my tea, and immediately began to cough violently.

Concerned, Mum banged me on the back. "What is it, child? Are you okay?"

More or less. The word *nice* in the context of our new headmistress had given me serious problems swallowing.

"She's horrendous," I said finally. "She's banned kissing on the school premises!"

For a moment Mum looked at me in astonishment, and then she started to laugh. When I didn't laugh, however, she stopped and asked rather unsurely, "You're joking, aren't you?"

I shook my head. Did I look like a Happy Hippo?

"Really?" Mum was **flabbergasted**. "You mean she really has declared a ban on kissing?"

I nodded.

Malt – Malz; gossip – Schwatz; to choke – ersticken; concerned – besorgt; flabbergasted – verblüfft

During Mum's last words Joker had come into the room, and immediately told her about the second horror. "You can take me away from school! She's demanding that I wear short trousers!"

Mum laughed again. "You in particular? What's she got against you?"

Joker told her the business about the school uniform. Whereupon Mum remembered that it had in fact been discussed at a PTA meeting. Bound to be one of Gracia's mother's ideas. That'd fit. Didn't she have a clothes shop as well?

"You did, I hope, oppose it then?" I just wanted to check.

Mum shook her head. "I don't really remember. There was a lot of discussion about it, but I had to leave early to meet a client and couldn't take part in the vote ..."

"Oh great!" I interrupted. "So it's your fault that Joker and I will soon have to change schools. You presumably don't believe we'll be going around in such a thing!"

"Not over my dead body!" my brother supported me.

Now, however, Mum turned **stroppy**. "You can get that idea out of your heads. There's no question of changing schools!"

"But they can't do it!" I cried **in anger**. "They're stamping on our rights!"

"Then do something about it."

---

stroppy – pampig; in anger – zornig

"What?"

Mum stood up to leave my room. She evidently didn't fancy **tackling** real problems now she'd finished work for the day. "No idea, but you'll think of something! After all, you're the children of a politician."

With these words she swept out of the room.

Great! I thought angrily. First of all she forgets about it all, then she **saddles** us with the responsibility. Typical adult. The world was so unfair!

My anger hadn't **abated** by the time I crawled into bed later on. I tossed and turned from one side to the other and came up with a **blazing** speech against Frau Biedermann's measures, particularly the kissing ban, when a text appeared on my mobile.

Kissing ban, Frau Biedermann,
You just don't start that sort of thing.
For students in love
have to kiss at school, too!
Kisses, my love, Meik!

I grinned, texted a ***g*** and **iluvu**, and rolled over to go to sleep. We'll beat her, I thought. We'll bring her down with humour! He who laughs last, laughs longest!

I'd slipped away from the school premises with the Pepper Dollies during our free period, which had, of course,

---

to tackle – angehen; to saddle – *hier:* aufhalsen;
to abate – sich legen; blazing – flammend; g = grin – grins;
iluvu = I love you

just been banned. Now we were sitting in our favourite café **slurping** lattes, a mega-trendy kind of milky coffee. A bit too expensive to do regularly, but today there was no alternative. What with all this frustration, you had to treat yourself to something nice.

Lea spooned up her **froth** and then asked with a creamy mouth, "Have you had any idea yet for what we can do about Frau Biedermann's barbaric leadership style? She'll pull it off, and will rob us of all the fun that's left to be had at school."

Somehow my hand felt in my trouser pocket for a crumpled-up bit of paper. What on earth was it? I pulled it out. Oh yes, it was that leaflet that Bastian, our gorgeous student head, had handed out yesterday with the info about the summer party. I put it on the table and flattened it out.

I had a **brainwave**. "What do you reckon to us turning the summer party into a protest event?"

"What do you mean turning it into a protest event?" Lea didn't get it straight away.

"Well, I don't know exactly, but somehow get publicity for our problem with Biedermann! There are always heaps of people there, and we can bring what's happening to us home to them."

Greetje was immediately full of enthusiasm. "Oh yes, let's start a clever campaign!"

"A comedy!"

"A theatre performance!"

---

to slurp – schlürfen; froth – Schaum;
brainwave – Eingebung, Geistesblitz

"Or we could sing and have a cabaret!"

"Maybe with a couple of kissing songs!"

I pulled my mobile out and read Meik's goodnight text to my friends.

"Brilliant!" said Lea. "We need more of that!"

"Exactly – and then we can have a revue about kissing. With songs and texts and lots of slapstick!"

"Coooooool!"

We were very excited about our idea. Now all we had to do was win the student heads over to it and then we could get stuck in.

"How much time have we got?"

"Six weeks."

I gesticulated to the waitress that we wanted to pay.

"Then let's get started! I have to do something. If I'm condemned to inactivity any longer, I'll go mad!"

"Wow, Kiki!" said Franzi, grinning. "That dynamic?"

Yes, everything within me was crying out for action!

"Come on," I **badgered**. "English is starting in a minute, and we'll find Meik and the student head at lunch break. If they go along with it, we're halfway there."

They did go along with it.

"A brilliant idea," agreed Meik, and Bastian immediately started wondering if we couldn't win over a couple of teachers to help us with the preparations and **rehearsals**. It was clear that everything had to be

---

to badger – *hier:* drängeln; rehearsal – Probe

professional if it were to impress other people and Frau Biedermann in particular. She'd see that we were capable of achieving something without her stupid measures and **threats** of punishment. Capable of achieving just because we wanted to achieve!

"Van Gogh's bound to join in when Greetje explains it all to him." Greetje nodded. Her father had come out on the students' side in the past, and in this case, it was in fact obvious where his sympathies would lie. With us!

"If we're going to rehearse songs, Uschi might help us," said Bastian. "She's a trained choir leader and is fantastic. I play the trumpet with her in the jazz combo."

Meik knew Uschi, too, and so we agreed that he and Bastian would **approach** her the next time the jazz combo met.

Then we wondered about who else to include in our secret preparation team.

"Anyone who joins in has to be able to sing or act, preferably both ..." I **mused** aloud.

"And be brave enough to appear in public."

"What about Mona?" suggested Meik.

Why didn't he just get a red handkerchief and wave it around in front of my eyes? As an aggression **trigger** it would have had the same effect.

Before I could talk him out of his stupid suggestion, however, Bastian said, "Is that the one with the great

---

threat – Androhung; to approach sb – auf jmdn. zugehen;
to muse – sinnieren; trigger – Auslöser

backside? I saw her at a fashion show. I reckon she'd do it."

I smiled somewhat sourly. After all, I'd been at exactly the same fashion show without my backside having made such a lasting impression.

But when Meik asked me, "What do you reckon, Kiki?" I nodded and mumbled, "I can talk to her."

And to myself I thought: And then perhaps I'll forget … purely by accident … After all, I had quite enough to remember.

"I'd also like to approach a couple of mates from my class. There are some really cool rappers. And I'm sure we could count our German teacher Schiller in. He's **ace**, with a real sense of humour."

It was true that I could only say that of our German teacher Wolfie to a limited **extent**. However, he was, of course, also acting head and for that reason not **trustworthy** in this matter. He'd be bound immediately to pass everything on to Frau Biedermann and then she'd just come up with another rule or possibly even ban the summer party.

"Should we get the PTA involved as well?" Bastian wondered. "Maybe they could free up a couple of euros to fit everyone out with costumes and **sheet music** …"

"No way," I immediately rejected the idea. "Gracia's mother is chairwoman, and she'd be bound to join forces with the headmistress. At any rate, Gracia has

---

ace – *hier:* spitze; extent – Ausmaß;
trustworthy – vertrauenswürdig; sheet music – Notenblätter

spent the last few days **bragging about** how fantastic her mother thinks Frau Biedermann's actions are."

We decided that we would each approach a couple of trustworthy people and get the aforementioned teachers to join in. And ten to 15 pupils should be enough for starters. We could always take a couple more into our confidence just before it all happened, and then we could send up the balloon: *Get this party started on a Saturday night!*

We had no idea of the amount of work we were saddling ourselves with. All the adults we approached promised to support us, but said that we had to do all the preparation ourselves first. Van Gogh said we should go to the town archives and find sources on the history of kissing. Uschi recommended that we go to the music library where there were bound to be all kinds of sound recordings with kissing songs on them, and Schiller advised Bastian to **search** through world literature, particularly drama and poetry, for kissing scenes. He was at least kind enough to give Bastian a list of tips as well.

And so a couple of days later I trudged along with the Pepper Dollies after school to the town archive. The sun was shining, and our enthusiasm for the whole thing wasn't the greatest after a long school day under Frau Biedermann's **reign of terror**. However, we wanted to finish what we'd started. We were not exactly in the best of **moods** when we entered the big, dark reading

---

to brag about sth – mit einer Sache angeben; to search – suchen; reign of terror – Schreckensherrschaft; mood – Laune

room. It had a **musty** smell of old books, and the ceiling-high, **densely** packed shelves compelled a certain amount of respect. In whispers, we were debating where best to begin our search when the door suddenly opened and in walked Meik and Mona.

"I thought you'd be here," he said in a relaxed manner. "Mona would love to join in. So I invited her to come right away."

He came over to me and planted a gentle kiss on my cheek. However, it only partly **quelled** my anger with him. How did he come to be dragging Mona around with him? Even if we were having a rather less intense relationship at the moment, that didn't mean she had to go found swinging her "great backside" on my territory! And anyway, what did Meik have to do with her? The pair of them had nothing to do with one another at school. Had he approached her on the bus? Was there perhaps some element of truth to Gracia's suspicions? Jealousy arose in me like **bile**. However, I bravely fought it back. Mona and Meik are fine, I told myself, and you really **couldn't set any store by** the words of a Slug.

Meik, of course, didn't fail to notice my reserve when he greeted me.

"Have you got a problem?" he asked as we followed Franzi – who hadn't exactly danced for joy at the sight of Mona – to the catalogue.

---

musty – muffig; dense – eng; to quell – besänftigen; bile – Galle; to not set any store by – nichts geben auf

"I hope I've got you!" I said, taking possession of him.

Meik gave me a sidelong look. "Are you jealous? About Mona, maybe?"

"**Speak up** a bit, why don't you!" I hissed, looking at Mona, who was a couple of paces behind us. All I needed was for him to show me up in front of her!

He gave me a questioning look, but then dropped the subject.

Franzi had **pounced on** the subject catalogue and had immediately started to look up *Kiss* and *Kissing*.

"Here!" she cried in excitement. "Here, here, here ... it is in fact a subject heading. Look, all sorts of books about kissing!"

Her not-exactly-quiet outburst brought the librarian onto the scene. The **initial bloom** of youth had long since faded, and she had a face like crumpled-up **parchment**.

I bet her skin rustles when she laughs, I thought. However, she didn't laugh but told us with a severe expression on her face not to make so much noise. Noise! Franzi's little outburst was hardly a noise. She should see us when we're really making a noise. Then the shelves would **wobble** and the **hefty tomes** would start doing the samba! All the same, we dampened our enthusiasm and our noise-levels and began to write down the shelf-marks of the most promising titles.

---

to speak up – lauter sprechen; to pounce on – sich stürzen auf;
initial bloom – erste Blüte; parchment – Pergament;
to wobble – wackeln; hefty tome – *hier:* Wälzer

"Listen," Mona whispered to me, "there's a book about chimpanzees' kissing rituals here. Do we want that as well?"

"Chimpanzees?" Presumably written by some behavioural scientist or another who had spent a couple of years mixing with them as Chief **Ape** in the **primeval forest**. "Isn't there anything similar about gorillas?" I replied quietly. "Then it would be easier to make the connection."

Mona had, of course, immediately got the **allusion** to Fabian and his gang of Gorillas. "Oh, everyone will work it out pretty easily," she said and made a note.

"Oh!" Franzi only just managed to suppress a cry of joy. "This sounds mega-brilliant, exactly what we need: *Kissing: A History from its* ***Origins*** *to the Present Day*."

"Give me the shelf-mark, and I'll go and find it right away," offered Mona. She wrote down the number of the book and set off for the relevant row of shelves, which was somewhere in the middle of the library on the gallery.

Mona climbed the steps. On the gallery was an elderly man, who was evidently highly interested in literature about kissing. By then, I had several numbers written on my list and so I decided to go up to the gallery as well. Meik was making for it, too. I had just climbed the first two steps when I suddenly heard loud voices coming from above me which once again disturbed the **solemn** atmosphere of the reading room.

---

ape – Affe; primeval forest – Urwald; allusion – Anspielung; origin – Ursprung; solemn – feierlich

"But we need that book really **urgently**," Mona was saying, and I could see her trying to take it off the elderly gentleman. He was evidently not **inclined** to hand it over.

Mona dived **randomly** into the shelf and pulled out a hefty tome. "You have this one," she said. "It's bound to be more exciting." She held it out to the man and at the same time with her other hand pulled at the book that the man was clutching.

This action evidently confused him for a moment. His **grasp** must have loosened, for I could see the book changing hands from him to Mona, who immediately pressed the other tome into his hands. But the very moment that he touched it, he noticed the trick that had been played on him, and stuffed the book back on the shelf. As he did so, he said rather angrily, "I don't want this book! I want the book back that I was reading. Give it to me at once, you **impudent** creature!"

However, the impudent creature had other plans. "What book? I haven't got a book!" With these words, she threw the offending book over the gallery balustrade straight into my arms.

I had no choice but to catch it, as I was **brought up** to treat books carefully. And allowing a book to go crashing onto a staircase from such a height really couldn't be described as careful.

I stared at the tome in my hands, still quite **at a loss**,

---

urgent – dringend; to be inclined – gewillt sein;
random – willkürlich; grasp – Griff; impudent – unverschämt;
to bring up – erziehen; to be at a loss – ratlos sein

when Mona came dashing down from the gallery and snatched the book from my hands. The man, now visibly angry, hastened after her, cursing as he did so – with some justification – about the **outrageous** behaviour of the youth of today. It didn't seem to impress Mona in the slightest, though. I saw her reach Meik and give him the book.

"Go on, hide it somewhere!" I heard her hissing.

As if at the touch of a button, he fled and disappeared between the lower bookshelves.

The man had reached Mona and grabbed her by the arm. "Where's the book? Give it back immediately!" he demanded loudly.

Of course all the commotion had attracted the librarian's attention as well.

Barely had she entered the field of vision of the man, who was now red with anger, when he pounced on her. Behind him, he was dragging Mona by the arm.

"Arrest this girl," he said. "She's stolen a book from me!"

The librarian looked at him in astonishment. "But, Herr Professor, she hasn't got a book. How on earth can she have stolen a book from you? And in any case, the books here don't belong to you but to everyone in the town ..."

The Professor felt misunderstood. "I didn't say she stole a book that belonged to me. I said she took a book away from me that I was reading. She threw it over the gallery onto the ground floor ..."

---

outrageous – empörend; barely – kaum

Now the librarian's eyes widened. Throwing books around was, of course, a barbaric act.

"Is that true?" she asked **sternly**.

Mona raised her shoulders and said with an innocent expression and a tone of deepest regret, "But I've not got any book. And I'd never throw books around either. You tell me: do I look like someone who could even so much as **bend** the page of a book? It makes me cry every time I see a dog-eared corner that some previous owner has made in one of my regulation school books."

I had to grin. What an actress! Although she was **exaggerating** quite a bit.

Meanwhile the Pepper Dollies had caught up with us. They were the only people in the library room, which was otherwise empty. When the librarian started to cross-examine them as witnesses, she, of course, got only one answer: "We didn't see any books flying off the gallery, honestly, we didn't."

And so the poor professor had no choice but to **despair** either **of** the youth of today or his own sanity.

Whichever one he'd decided to despair of, it didn't, however, keep him any longer at the place of his **defeat**. He left the town archive saying angrily, "You've not heard the last of this! I'm going to **complain** to your superiors!"

The librarian shook her head as she watched him go.

---

stern – streng; to bend – *hier:* knicken;
to exaggerate – übertreiben; to despair of – verzweifeln an;
defeat – Niederlage; to complain – sich beschweren

"So sad," she said. "He's never been that confused before. He's really **getting on** a bit, the poor chap."

Then she turned to us. "We're closing in a minute. If you want to borrow anything, you need to do it now."

Franzi had already taken a small heap of books to the **issue desk**, and the librarian went over to scan them in. As she did so she looked kind of embarrassed, presumably on account of the racy topic. "What do you want with all these books?" she asked finally, evidently unable to contain her curiosity any longer.

"Erm ... well ..." said Franzi. "A school project."

Astonishment. "The things you learn at school nowadays!"

"Where did you hide the book?" Mona **quizzed** Meik as to the whereabouts of the hard-won tome. "Go on, go and fetch it! They're shutting any minute now. Do you think I made such a performance just for it to lie around mouldering away somewhere?"

My goodness, didn't that girl **have a gob on her**.

It presumably didn't appeal to Meik much either, for he suddenly grabbed my hand and pulled me between the bookshelves. When he stopped, however, he seemed at a loss. "Hmm, I thought I'd hidden it somewhere in between the other books."

Oh great.

"Where is it?" I asked impatiently, trying to remember what the book had looked like.

---

to get on – *hier:* alt werden;
issue desk – Ausleihe; to quiz – fragen;
to have a gob on you – eine freche Schnauze haben

"The title was *A History of Kissing* or something ..."

But how mega-stupid just to stuff the book onto a shelf. We'd never find it again amidst all these millions of books!

"Come on, forget it," I was about to say resignedly when Meik cried **in delight**, "Got it! Got it! Eureka! I knew I'd hidden it here!"

The librarian did then scan the book, **albeit** with a rather mistrustful look. We were about to take it away when she put her hand on it and asked, "How old are you, actually?"

"Thirteen," I said, and Meik replied, "Sixteen."

"Then I'm afraid I can't lend you the book. It's not **suitable** for children under eighteen."

"Eh?"

We stared at one another **in bewilderment**. What on earth could be 18-certificate about a book on the history of kissing? It didn't even have any pictures.

The librarian didn't enter into any discussion about it. "There's a note here that says the book can only be lent out to adults, and there will be a reason for it."

Now she **frowned** so sternly that I thought I could in fact hear her skin rustling. "I'm sorry."

She took the book from the issue desk and stood up decisively.

"She's presumably going to put it back in the poison cabinet!"

---

in delight – erfreut; albeit – wenn auch; suitable – geeignet;
in bewilderment – verblüfft; to frown – die Stirn runzeln

"What a pity," said Mona. "And now I can see why that old grandpa was so keen on it."

Giggling, we left the town archive. Once outside the library, we were still killing ourselves laughing.

"A real pity, Mona!" Meik finally gasped, out of breath. "But the idea was brilliant, even if it didn't work out!" And to me and the Pepper Dollies he said, "Do you see now why Mona absolutely has to be involved? She has the craziest ideas!"

Squabbles with stupid cows

"Let me tell you, something's not right there," declared Franzi during our evening phoning session. "Meik is showing decidedly too much interest in Mona."

Now she was at it as well. But what could I do? After all, Meik's jealousy had made him impossible during the fashion show. I didn't want to behave that stupidly now. And anyway, I was above such **petty** feelings. But was I really? No! I wasn't! I was boiling with anger and almost eaten up with fury! "Franzi, I'll kill him if he doesn't keep his hands off Mona!"

"Oh, rubbish! Work out first whether he's worth it! If so, then fight for him. If not, then ... well, you know."

When I was lying in bed and my mobile announced Meik's evening text, I read the message somewhat **hesitantly**.

The book business was the best thing that's happened for weeks, he wrote. *Just discovered I can't kiss you via mobile! Boo!:-x Sweet dreams all the same. Meik.*

---

squabble – Zank, Streit; petty – kleinlich;
hesitant – zögernd

The best thing that's happened for weeks? And who did he have to thank for that? Mona! I drummed my **fists** angrily into my pillow. It was clear that I'd have to come up with an idea. Was he worth it? Of course he was! The problem wasn't him, but Mona!

So long as she was running around **unattached**, she was a risk. It was obvious that **in the long run** no boy could resist the charm that she constantly **exuded**.

Suddenly it was all crystal clear. Someone had to **ensnare** Mona and stop her turning the heads of all the boys in our school! What kind of ensnaring could it be? Something that would turn off all the other boys. In that case, there was only one kind of ensnaring: love! A steady relationship. It was quite simple: Mona needed a boyfriend! Only then would I have my peace restored. Yes indeed! If I weren't to die a miserable death by jealousy, I had to **matchmake** her with somebody. But with whom?

I grabbed my mobile again and called Franzi. It was a while before her sleepy voice answered.

"Sorry, Franzi, don't be angry with me, it's really, really urgent and ... because ... you said I should fight for Meik ... that's what you said ..."

Franzi cleared her throat. "What I actually meant is that you should **dump** him!"

---

fist – Faust; unattached – ungebunden;
in the long run – dauerhaft; to exude – *hier:* versprühen;
to ensnare – umgarnen; to matchmake – verkuppeln;
to dump sb – *hier:* jmdm. den Laufpass geben

I **contradicted** her. "You don't really mean that! You're only saying that because you're fed up with me for waking you up ..."

"Fed up is an understatement ..."

"Oh Franzi, you know you're my best friend. Who else am I **supposed to** talk to about such a serious problem?"

Now she felt **flattered**. "Go on then, spit it out. What's so urgent?"

I took a deep breath. "Well, I know how to eliminate Mona as a risk factor."

"Risk factor is good. So's eliminate. How, then?"

"We have to matchmake her with someone. If she's in safe hands, she can't be a danger to us any more."

Franzi giggled non-stop. She finally stopped, drew breath, and said, "And you reckon she'll just let herself be **paired off** with someone?"

"Yes, no kidding, I reckon she will," I said **snottily**, as she was making a joke out of my idea. I was, you see, very serious about it. "I'll prove it to you! In three weeks she'll have a boyfriend or I'll let her have Meik."

"Great," said Franzi, yawning widely. "**It's a bet**!"

When I lay back against my beaten-up pillow, I had the stupid feeling that I'd played a trick on myself.

---

to contradict – widersprechen;
to be supposed to do sth – etwas tun sollen;
flattered – geschmeichelt; to pair off – verkuppeln;
snotty – patzig; It's a bet. – Die Wette gilt.

Next morning, however, the world looked nicer once again. When I met my friends at the Altstadt market, we had another good laugh about the kiss-**addict** grandpa.

The morning was stuffed full of **compulsory** lessons but during the afternoon we had clubs, and we got van Gogh's permission to **withdraw** for a secret meeting in the equipment store behind the art room.

"What do you reckon to us putting up huge kissing ban signs all over the school premises for the summer party?" I suggested.

An idea that was enthusiastically **seized upon**. And so we dragged along **cardboard** and masses of red paint. It was, admittedly, a bit of a **squeeze**, and you could hardly move without bumping into a table or one of the wobbly low-down shelves on which we'd deposited our equipment and paint.

"Watch out!" Fabian's warning cry came too late. A shelf started to wobble and tipped over. Paintbrushes, tins of paint and buckets clattered to the floor, together with Raffi. When the unfortunate creature re-emerged from the **tangle** of equipment, his hands and clothes were as red as his ears.

"Under the shower, quick!" said Franzi in a **maternal** voice. "It's acrylic paint, so it'll wash off in water so long as it's still wet."

---

addict – süchtig; compulsory – Pflicht-;
to withdraw – zurückziehen; to seize upon – aufgreifen;
cardboard – Karton; squeeze – Enge;
tangle – Durcheinander, Gewirr; maternal – mütterlich

I giggled. Then he could at least take his time with his ears, as I reckoned that Raffi was by no means dry behind them. And quite **apart from that**, their colour would anyway resist all attempts to clean it off.

I was right. When he returned in his jogging **gear**, his ears were still as red as fire alarms. As always, I couldn't understand what Franzi saw in this **randy** little **dwarf**. He evidently **enabled** her to live out her prematurely maternal instincts. Probably because, unlike me, she wasn't landed with a younger brother. That kind of thing **toughens** you **up**. Oh well, so what, if it meant she was going to mother me a bit less. And he was actually kind of cute.

We were still in the process of sorting out Raffi's mishap in a rather rough and ready way when the first curious onlookers appeared. The noise of the collapsing shelf had, of course, been **audible** in the art room. That was, however, not at all in the spirit of the thing, and this very fact alone made me wish that Raffi would just get lost.

"What are you up to in here?" the Slugs immediately wanted to know, Gracia in particular. "I thought this was the art club. Doesn't that **apply to** you?"

I looked at her with annoyance, because I hate people who are constantly sticking their nose into other peo-

---

apart from that – davon abgesehen; gear – Zeug, *hier:* Anzug;
randy – scharf, geil; dwarf – Zwerg;
to enable sb to do sth – jmdm. etwas ermöglichen;
to toughen up – abhärten; audible – hörbar;
to apply to – gelten für

ple's business, and chucked a red-**soaked** paper towel at her which I'd just used to wipe paint off the table. "Push off," I said. "This is **a closed shop**."

She jumped aside and my **missile** hit the door. It slid down leaving a thick red **trail** behind it.

"Yuck! Is there a happening going on in here?!" screeched Daphne next to her.

"Nah, a vampire party!" Mona said drily. Then she pulled a face, bared her teeth and snapped, "Blooooooood!"

Of course van Gogh appeared shortly afterwards to make sure everything was alright.

"Oh! What's been going on here?" he cried in astonishment, looking sharply at Greetje as if he were saying, Well, out with it, daughter!

Greetje understood his look and tried to explain, but Gracia interrupted her and said rather impudently to van Gogh, "Why don't they have to take part in the art club? Why can they hang around here making a mess without anyone **bothering**? I don't think Frau Biedermann would think much of this."

Frau Biedermann! So now she was **crawling around** her! Well, then we had to **be on our guard**.

I was just about to come up with a suitable **riposte**

---

soaked – getränkt; a closed shop – geschlossene Gesellschaft;
missile – *hier:* Wurfgeschoss; trail – Spur;
to bother – sich kümmern;
to crawl around sb – *hier:* sich bei jmdm. einschleimen;
to be on one's guard – auf der Hut sein; riposte – Erwiderung

when van Gogh **beat me to** it. "I am bothered," he said quietly. "I just have a different way of showing it. So go back to the art room, please, and get on with *your* work so that this group here can get on with *theirs*."

Gracia tossed back her head and continued to make trouble. "Work? What's this mess got to do with work?"

"Look for yourself: we're painting the equipment room ..." Franzi said **pertly**.

"And Raffi as well, eh?" countered Daphne.

"Of course," said Mona. "We're always willing to listen to special requests."

She took a dripping paintbrush and moved aggressively towards Daphne.

The latter sprang back in horror, thereby colliding with Gracia, who pushed her away with a "Watch out!", right back into Mona's paintbrush. Splat! It got her in the face, and Mona got some on her arm as well.

Haha! It looked **ethnic**, like Ogallala war-paint or something.

Had I perhaps giggled out loud about the misfortune of my fellow pupil? Shame on me. In that case, it served me right when Gracia said rudely, "You won't be laughing for much longer."

"Oh, why's that? I have such a sunny disposition."

By now Gracia had turned bright red without needing any added paint. She's going to explode any moment now, I thought, when it all came bursting out of

---

to beat sb to sth – jmdm. bei etwas zuvorkommen;
pert – schnippisch; ethnic – folkloristisch

her. "You needn't show off. And so far as your laughing about Mona's **sludgy** mess is concerned – I hardly think you'd be laughing about it if you knew what I know ..."

I sat up and took notice. "What do you know?"

"Well, for example, that Mona's trying to get off with your guy ..."

"You're lying!"

"... and he's trying to get off with her!" The last words slid off her lips like a trail of slime. Yuck! That girl could be so disgusting. But what I'd heard was even worse. I stared at Gracia, then at Mona.

The latter dropped her paintbrush. Didn't she look **hideously** guilty? "Let me explain, Kiki ..." she said.

So it was true! I'd known it all along! I bit my lip in order not to yell at her. With two steps I was at the door; I swept Gracia aside with a violent arm movement, and ran off through the art room.

In the girls' loos, I locked myself in a **cubicle** and began to **sob** non-stop. So it was true, true, true!!! They'd all been right. I was the stupid cow who'd **lost her bearings** again. The birds were singing it from the rooftops, the frogs were croaking it in the **ponds**, the insects were chirping it in the grass, and I – it took a Slug to open my eyes!

Mona and Meik, Meik and Mona! How could they have **deceived** me without my noticing!

---

sludgy – schmierig; hideous – furchtbar;
cubicle – Kabine; to sob – schluchzen;
to have lost one's bearings – nicht mehr aus noch ein wissen;
pond – Teich; to deceive – hintergehen

I **crouched** on the loo seat, and tears poured down my face. I stared at the cubicle door, which was completely covered with filthy graffiti. The letters swam before my eyes. Thank God, because I couldn't do with the absurd humour of my fellow pupils on top of everything else. Nor with the linked hearts either with or without initials. Hadn't I recently scratched one with K&M on the door myself? Life was hideous, completely hideous ...

I heard voices in the loos. Someone tried the handle of my cubicle door.

"Kiki? Are you in there? Don't be silly! You surely don't believe Gracia?"

Me? Believe Gracia? Of course I didn't; you couldn't believe a Slug ... but I did believe her! Oh **curses!** I believed her! What possible reason could she have to lie to me? To lie to me about Meik and Mona of all things? I'd secretly feared it the whole time. Even at the fashion show I'd asked myself whether Meik was really leaning against the column in the city centre to watch me, or whether he wasn't perhaps watching Mona, too. Gracia simply confirmed Franzi's suspicions and my secret **anxieties**.

"Kiki" – that was Mona's voice. "Kiki, you surely don't believe the rubbish that Gracia just came out with about me and Meik? I thought we were friends ..."

Friends? Mona and me? I had in fact thought so after the fashion show, but now ...

"Kiki, come out. You surely don't want to give Gra-

---

to crouch – kauern; Curses! – Verdammt!;
anxiety – Befürchtung

cia this triumph! And what's Meik going to think?" That was Lea.

And Franzi said, "It's bound not to be the way Gracia says it is."

Then it's something different, I thought, but there's still going to be a **grain** of truth in it. Who knows whether they squeeze up close somewhere other than on the bus. Gracia was bound to have seen them somewhere!

Someone rattled the door handle again. "Open up, Kiki!" That was Greetje. Well, there seemed to be a real party going on in the girls' loos. "Biedermann's on her way. You don't want her to find you!"

No, I really didn't want that. But I was practically paralysed, incapable of moving. All I could do was stare into space, and what I saw with my inner eye was shattered **remains**. And not the kind of broken china you get at a **hen** or **stag night**, but the smashed remains of my first relationship!

"Kiki," Mona said again. "Kiki, I **swear** there's nothing going on between Meik and me. I like him, he likes me, but that's it! Believe me ... I don't love him!"

"Interesting, interesting!"

Was I hearing correctly? That was Meik's slightly ironic intonation. What on earth was he doing in the girls' loos?

The very next moment, someone else wanted to

---

grain – *hier:* Körnchen; remains – Überbleibsel;
hen/stag night – Junggesellinnen-/Junggesellenabschied;
to swear – schwören

know that, too. Our new headmistress's voice cut through the room. "What is this boy here doing in the girls' toilets? I demand an immediate explanation!"

My tears stopped with shock. Oh God, how was Meik going to get himself out of this mess? After the two warnings about snogging, he'd be bound to get a black mark on his report if he couldn't talk himself out of this one. Old solidarity was awakened in me. I had to help him. I sprang up, unlocked the door, and fell out. I must have looked so **wretched** that nobody could doubt the truth of my words as I stammered, "I, I … I don't feel well, and Meik's the school **first-aider**, Franziska fetched him … I …"

I felt around for something to hold onto, and then sank in an almost perfect **faint** into Franzi's arms.

Meik, of course, immediately seized the opportunity to remove himself and then me from the scene. He felt my pulse and then said, "I'll take her to the sick-room. Her **circulation**'s a bit unstable."

He picked me up in his arms and carried me past Frau Biedermann, who was **genuinely** irritated for the first time.

"Is she having her period?" I heard Frau Biedermann asking, before the door which Franzi had been holding open banged shut behind us. I shut my eyes. We were saved – for the time being.

Well, that was yet another operation and a half!, I

---

wretched – erbärmlich; first-aider – Ersthelfer; faint – Ohnmacht; circulation – Kreislauf; genuine – echt

thought, and sighed. Typical Kiki. My goodness, I'd **put my foot in it** a dozen times for the price of one. It would have been totally understandable if Meik had now had enough and suddenly decided to transfer his affections from me to Mona.

However, he didn't – at least not for the moment. Once we'd rounded the next corner, I had immediately jumped out of his arms, but he insisted on actually taking me to the sick-room.

"But I'm not ill!" I said, and tried to explain to him that I'd only put on that performance to save him from Biedermann.

"But you look ill," he said **obstinately**. "You can freshen up a bit in the sick-room."

Oh well, it couldn't do any **harm**.

One look in the little, half clouded-over mirror in the sick-room confirmed one hundred percent what Meik had said. **For heaven's sake**, I really couldn't go out in public looking like that! I was **tousled** and tear-stained and, to **cap it all**, my face, hair and hands were spattered in red paint. A highly dramatic sight. Perhaps Frau Biedermann had taken the paint for blood? Oh horrors! What on earth must she think of me now?!

After my clean-up operation, I wanted to leave the sick-room straight away, but Meik pulled me down onto the sick-bed. I sat down hesitantly. He put his arm round

---

to put one's foot in it – ins Fettnäpfchen treten; obstinate – stur; to do harm – schaden; for heaven's sake – um Himmels willen; tousled – zerzaust; to cap it all – zu allem Überfluss

me and began to stroke me gently. So who had brought him to the girls' loos?

"Greetje. I was just with Uschi and the jazz combo."

Oh no, how embarrassing!

"No, it wasn't. Of course she didn't say you were sitting on the loo and crying."

Well, that was at least something. But it was embarrassing enough anyway.

"I wasn't crying."

He looked at me in astonishment. "Oh?!"

We were silent.

"So, are you going to let on about what was actually the matter? What on earth makes you think I don't love you?" he asked after a while.

I snuggled up in his arms. Yes, what did make me think it? I had no desire to tell him now about Gracia and my jealousy, so I just said **sheepishly**, "So you do love only me?"

"What a silly question," he said, stroking my hair which was still partly **damp**. "Everything's okay between us – so long as you don't make it complicated ..."

Was I doing that?

Over the next few days, the kissing club really got going. Student heads and year reps and not least Meik had founded a **conspiratorial** organisation and had actually managed to get the leader of the jazz combo to take on the musical rehearsals.

---

sheepish – verlegen; damp – feucht; conspiratorial – konspirativ

"Call me Uschi," she'd said, all **chilled out**, the first time we'd met. She was a small, energetic person who knew her subject inside out. Short brown hair and strange flowing clothes in a kind of hippy style made for a rather **peculiar** contrast. However, when you looked into her bright, sparkling eyes and heard her **astonishingly** deep and gentle voice, it all kind of fitted together. Next to van Gogh, she looked like a little bird, but that was quite **fitting** for a music teacher.

By now, there were 15 of us who were actively supported by the jazz combo. All the Pepper Dollies were, of course, included, plus a couple of Meik's mates from his year, and Mariam, Bastian and a couple of other year reps. Unfortunately, it also included Fabian, our year rep and chief Gorilla. And Franzi had refused to **abandon** the idea of dragging Raffi along.

I thought it was great that we'd set up a club that **spanned** all the year-groups. It was a good way to get to know some of the older kids. However, I found it less **delightful** that Mona was part of the club, since I still felt that she was my competitor in whatever we did. Franzi was right. We were just too similar to be real friends. It wasn't just that we shared many of the same interests; unfortunately, we also shared our taste in boys, and this couldn't work in the long run. And the way things were

---

chilled out – entspannt; peculiar – seltsam;
astonishing – erstaunlich; fitting – passend;
to abandon – aufgeben; to span – umfassen;
delightful – erfreulich

developing at the moment, all alarms were **on red alert**. Kiki, watch out!, it meant. Mona's **poaching** in your territory.

So far as the revue was concerned, I had to admit, however, that Mona was a bonus in terms of creativity and providing ideas. It was her idea, for example, to **string together** little kissing scenes of great lovers from films and history in a revue style.

"Oh cool," said Fabian, pleased. "Then we can roll Mona up in a **rug** and I'll be Julius Caesar who unrolls her and kisses her."

"Did he actually do that?" I asked sceptically.

But it evidently sounded as if I were **begrudging** Mona a kiss from Fabian, as he said ironically, "If not, then we can just re-write history a bit – if, of course, Kiki doesn't object." And turning to me, he asked, "Or do you just want to **reclaim** the role for yourself?"

Pah! Had he **lost his marbles**? They could do it by all means – who was keen on Gorilla kisses? I certainly wasn't.

On the other hand, Mona seemed to be using every trick in the book to **bag** herself the most attractive roles.

---

to be on red alert – in höchster Alarmbereitschaft sein;
to poach – wildern; to string together – aneinanderhängen;
rug – Teppich; to begrudge sb sth – jmdm. etwas nicht gönnen;
to reclaim – beanspruchen;
to lose one's marbles – den Verstand verlieren;
to bag oneself sth – sich etwas unter den Nagel reißen

One morning she appeared with her hair **dyed** totally red.

"My goodness!" gasped Greetje, who even at the best of times regarded any **major** interference in the **divine** order as sacrilege. "Doesn't she look crazy?"

And Gracia said smugly, "If you want to **walk the streets**, you don't need to go to school."

Whereupon Mona replied drily, "Nor do you, if you want to have the kind of petit bourgeois existence you've had so far! By the way, no hairstyle's ever going to work with that **straw**-blond hair of yours, because you've not just got straw on your head but *in* it as well. So far as any kind of lifestyle's concerned, you're a complete **dead loss**!"

The following sports lesson went quite well apart from a little incident with Lydia, who yet again couldn't pass the ball during basketball and even tried to foul me. But she'd have to be a lot sharper than that! I was subtly blocking her and before she noticed properly, she slipped and landed at Fabian's feet. He caught the ball that slid away from her and placed it coolly into the basket with no effort at all. Then he **bent down** to her, gallantly offered her his hand, and said, "No need to throw yourself at my feet. The ball on its own would have been quite **sufficient**."

---

to dye – färben; major – größer; divine – göttlich;
to walk the streets – auf den Strich gehen; straw – Stroh;
to be a dead loss – *hier:* eine Nullnummer sein;
to bend down – sich hinunterbeugen; sufficient – ausreichend

Lydia turned **chalk**-white with **fury**, and when she recovered, she hissed to me angrily, "It's not over yet! You can bet your life on it!"

Were there such things as poisonous Slugs? If not, we'd soon have to **re-name** the Slugs as some creature more suitable!

But you shouldn't **underestimate** your enemies. The Slug-empire immediately struck back.

When I unsuspectingly went to the toilet at the end of the class, Lydia, Daphne and Gracia were already standing in the **anteroom**, whispering excitedly to one another. When I entered, they abruptly stopped their conversation. They stared at me, started to whisper again, and then suddenly made simultaneously for the cubicles, leaving only one for me. Whatever. One was quite enough.

I sat down and stared at the cubicle door, lost in thought. My heart and biorhythm stopped. My eyes almost popped out of my head, and an inarticulate **gasp** escaped from my throat, which suddenly had a huge lump in it. Just as if I'd swallowed my own mega-swollen **uvula**.

On the cubicle door, which had only recently been repainted, there was a prominent lipstick heart in which it said: *Mona + Meik*!

How incredibly mean! How could Mona do something like that to me? To my face, she was innocently

---

chalk – Kreide; fury – Wut; to re-name – umtaufen;
to underestimate – unterschätzen; anteroom – Vorraum;
gasp – Keuchen; uvula – Zäpfchen

saying, "I don't love Meik", and behind my back, she was painting stuff like this on the loo door!

But why Mona? an inner voice suddenly asked me as the Slugs' giggling **wafted over** to me from the anteroom of the toilets. These stupid cows could have planned it. Of course it stank of Lydia, Gracia and Daphne taking revenge on Mona and me. It was all a pre-arranged trick to play us off against one another. They'd **engineered** it very cleverly, and now they were standing in the **basin** area waiting for me to come out so they could have a laugh at my misery. Well, they were in for a surprise. I was going to spoil their fun.

I pulled some loo paper off the roll and wiped the lipstick heart off the cubicle door.

"Whoops," I said as I emerged from the cubicle, and put the lipstick-smeared paper on the side of the basin by Daphne. "One of you spilt lipstick in my loo. I've already wiped it up, but you can dispose of your own rubbish!"

The giggling had at least stopped. It must have been them, I thought, though I couldn't, of course, be entirely sure. Whatever!

Whatever was up with this story, lies or not, something finally had to be done.

When I then discovered in the kissing club that Mona had obviously dyed her hair red only in order to get the role of Scarlett O'Hara and fall into the arms of Meik alias Rhett Butler in the *Gone With The Wind* scene, I'd

---

to waft over – dringen; to engineer – aushecken;
basin – Waschbecken

decided one thing for sure: Mona had to be taken out of circulation. She needed a boyfriend who would stop her from seeing the entire school as one big **cattle** market. And, as I'd bet with Franzi, I'd find her one right away.

The only question was: how?!

---

cattle – Vieh

Cupid on the Internet

That evening I was sitting at the computer playing Algeblaster, an educational game that my father liked and which was teaching me the basics of algebra. But I couldn't concentrate. I stared at the brightly coloured aliens and thought about other things entirely.

What a misunderstanding! Yet I didn't want to make my relationship with Meik all complicated. On the contrary! I wanted everything to be clear and **straightforward**. And that's what I'd **bring about** for once and for all. Whatever Meik and Mona said, I'd started to trust nobody but the Pepper Dollies. I'd only be reassured once Mona was in safe hands. And that would soon be the case. Three weeks: pah! I'd find a taker for her far more quickly than that. I also knew already who it would be, and I'd just had an idea about how to do it. The computer was exactly the right medium to make them fall in love with one another in a contemporary

---

Cupid – Amor;
straightforward – ehrlich; to bring about – zuwege bringen

and anonymous way. So much for bows and arrows! Cupid worked via e-mail nowadays!

I closed my programme and went online. "Joker, can you help me!?" I called for my highly talented brother's help. After all, why else have such a computer freak in the family?

He shuffled along in his usual leisurely **gait**. He presumably couldn't walk any faster in his over-long and wide jeans without falling flat on his face. "What's up?" he asked casually.

"Can you set up an e-mail address for me?" I asked. "One that means I'd stay anonymous."

"No problemo. What do you want to be called?" He sat at the PC and went to a provider's homepage.

"Will my name and address really not be sent with the e-mails?"

He shook his head. "You can give an invented name."

A mask appeared on the screen into which I only needed to enter a few bits of information.

"Fill that in. If you get stuck, give me a shout. I have to watch Dragon Ball." He shuffled off.

"No malt beer today?" I asked.

"But of course." He grinned. "You think I can save the rainforest on that stuff?"

"Beer is beer," I said and started to fill in the information.

Now I just needed a chic name for the address, and a cool password. I pondered. The name had to suit Mona's out-of-the-ordinary personality.

---

gait – Gang

Hmm. I didn't actually know that much about her. Stylish, self-confident, cheeky as anything, and evidently every boy's dream. There we have it: *Boy's Dream*.

Or did that sound too **conceited**? Might that rather turn people off? Hmm, maybe it would sound like some **porn**-site was behind it. Not so great. I pondered further. Something romantic wouldn't be bad, I thought, and a hint of secrecy; after all, I wanted to make the guy curious about Mona. And he should suspect a bit that she's behind it. Mona ... Monalisa ... heavens above, it couldn't be so hard to think of a suitable name for an e-mail address! And then suddenly it hit me: Monalieschen! That sounded pretty cool, didn't it? **Reminiscent of** the secret smile of Monalisa, contains Mona's name and a little **knowing nod**. That way nobody would think she was being arrogant, but a bit self-ironic. Fantastic.

But then I thought it might be a bit too direct after all. The connection between Monalieschen and Mona was a little obvious after all. True, I didn't want to wait forever for the guy to work out who she was, but a bit more mystery wouldn't **go amiss**. Better to go for just M-lieschen.

As a password I inserted *Aphrodite*. What could be more fitting than the goddess of love! So, it was done.

---

conceited – eingebildet; porn – Porno ;
to be reminiscent of – an etwas erinnern;
a knowing nod – ein Augenzwinkern;
to go amiss – *hier:* schaden

Now I just had to wait for confirmation and then I could get stuck in.

Before long, it was all sorted. My new mailbox was set up. I could get started. Franzi would be amazed by how quickly I'd paired Mona off. And, what's more, with our student head – with Bastian.

I **dug** the student council leaflet out of my rucksack. On it was Bastian's e-mail address. Then I found a greetings card: a hot cabriolet with two lovers on a **steep** rock at sunset. Cars were never a bad idea with boys. My fingers trembling slightly, I typed Bastian's address in: *Bastinochild@gmx.de*. Now all I needed was a message that would turn him on.

But what would turn on a 16-year-old student head? If I barely knew Mona, I didn't know him at all.

Given the kitschy card, a humorous **antidote** was undoubtedly called for. Could I try a witty love-poem? I'd found all sorts of them for our revue. Ah yes, that would give the whole thing a quasi-businesslike air. He could **relate** it **to** himself, but didn't have to. It was playing with fire without setting light to everything all at once.

I went over to my Pop Sofa and **sifted through** the mountain of poetry. Ringelnatz, Morgenstern, Tucholsky, Loriot ...

All of them were almost too funny. I stopped. There, Günter Kunert. Never heard of him, but the poem was cool. Mega-suitable. I took the text and wrote it beneath the card:

---

to dig – graben; steep – steil; antidote – *hier:* Kontrapunkt; to relate to – beziehen auf; to sift through – durchgehen

Together in the car
Driving through deserted streets
Shattered ***wasps*** *on the windscreen*
Splashing rain
Sun and darkness
And more sun: Exchanging
few words. ***Absent***
togetherness. Carefree.
Happiness.

I read it through once more. Brilliant, truly brilliant. It couldn't be more fitting. Not to the card or to the situation. *Exchanging few words. Absent togetherness.* Ha! How mega-brilliant and so nicely **ambiguous** and kind of a bit vague. It'd make him curious, at any rate. Simply ideal for a first approach. Okay, so the squashed wasps on the windscreen were perhaps a bit **gross**, but nothing was perfect. On the other hand, I could just delete that bit. No sooner said than done. It was much shorter and snappier like that. Better to leave the rain out, too. Sun was enough. Otherwise he'd think that M-lieschen was a depressive.

That sounded much better. I left the deserted streets in. I had no idea what the poet meant by it, but it sounded mysterious. So, let's read it through again. Great. Now a chic **font** colour. I chose a dark red. Well, let's see what it looked like beneath the card. I clicked on "preview". Fantastic. It was bound to **blow his mind**!

---

wasp – Wespe; absent – abwesend; ambiguous – zweideutig;
gross – krass; font – Schrift;
to blow one's mind – jmdn. umhauen

Then, as I moved the cursor over "send", I shivered slightly all over. Should I really do it? That sort of thing really wasn't done. Scruples flew in. But then my inner coach gave me a kick. Things couldn't go on like this, and Bastian was after all a pretty good guy. If I managed to get him interested in Mona, she should be happy. My index finger pressed the left-click mouse button. The e-mail had gone. M-lieschen to Bastinochild. What had I done?

There was a noise at the front door and Snuffles started yapping.

I looked at the clock. It had to be Dad. He'd got the evening train from Berlin again. When I went out of my bedroom and into the hall, his laptop was standing there and his coat was on the bench. A babble of voices was coming from the kitchen. Dad was sitting at the breakfast bar with a welcome-home drink – was he trying to save the rainforest as well?

Mum was frying eggs, and Joker was **addressing** a **torrent** of words to my father. The topic was – how could it be anything else? – the new headmistress and her gross debut at school. Dad had circles under his eyes and didn't look capable of taking very much in.

"It won't be so bad," he said **dully**, and it was obvious that he couldn't face discussions about suitable and unsuitable headmistresses after a week-long session in parliament.

---

to address – richten an; torrent – Sturzbach; dull – lustlos

All the same, at least the kissing ban ought to be put on the table. After all, I'd promised my friends that I'd find out whether it was compatible with the **Basic Law**.

But Mum blocked me. "Not today, Kiki, Dad's exhausted, and it's time for you to go to bed. It'll keep till tomorrow."

We went off to our rooms, rather **offended**. I slipped into my pyjamas and went into the bathroom. When I returned, curiosity drove me to the computer again after all. Had Bastian already read the card?

I went to the inbox. Yes indeed. There was the message: *Your greetings card to Bastinochild was received.* Hmm. Five past ten this evening. That was ten minutes ago. Enough time to write back? I felt quite **jumpy**. But he was doubtless totally confused. He was bound to be wondering who'd written him that e-mail. Would he think of Mona? It was in fact pretty obvious. Though M-lieschen could mean lots of things. Oh **crikey!** Maybe he thought it was Mariam. She was, after all, student head in his parallel class, and he knew her from the school council. How stupid! Yet again, I hadn't thought long and hard enough about it. And what if Bastian already had a girlfriend? Oh no, how embarrassing, I hadn't remotely considered that. Whoops! Just as I was feeling **thoroughly** ashamed of myself, an e-mail appeared. *Bastinochild to M-lieschen.*

Basic Law – Grundgesetz; offended – beleidigt;
jumpy – nervös; Crikey! – Mensch!;
thorough – gründlich

I **trembled** with stress right down to my **entrails**. What had he written?

I didn't **dare** to open the e-mail, but jumped off my chair and walked up and down my bedroom a couple of times. In all the panic, I almost trod on Snuffles, who had settled down for the night right by my bed.

I have to know, I said to myself, I can't sleep without knowing what he's written. *For goodness' sake, then open it,* said my inner coach. I sat down at the computer again. At least Bastian had sent a greetings card as well. That was probably why he'd taken so long to reply. He had to find something **equally** brilliant. I didn't care why now. I wanted to know what was going on, and opened the e-mail.

Eek! A big fat kiss-shaped mouth **smacked its lips** at me from the screen. The card was animated! Fantastic! Where had he dug that up from? After delivering the smacker, the mouth disappeared and a bright text appeared:

Kissing can't be forbidden.
That's why we're fighting together
against such dead-loss teachers
until the sun shines again.
I've not got a driving licence yet,
So I can't drive around with you.
But I'd like to be with you,
To lose myself in sunshine!

---

to tremble – zittern;
entrails – Eingeweide; to dare – wagen; equal – gleich;
to smack one's lips – schmatzen

Are you the girl I think you are?
Bastian

I had read the lines breathlessly and was still trembling. My God, was he ever sweet! So who did he reckon it was? Mona, no doubt. But he mustn't approach her yet under any **circumstances**. I had to reply to him. My fingers were already gliding over keyboard.

Thanks for replying. I'm really glad you did, but let me keep my secret for a bit longer. Even if you think you know who I am, don't approach me at school. I have my reasons. It's not yet time.
Me

I sent the e-mail and closed the **application**, still completely **churned up**. After these lines, he'd be bound not to approach Mona and I had time to work out what should happen next with this whole business.

You're nuts, girl, my inner governess **grouched** as I lay in bed, slowly coming to my senses. *Now you've gone completely mad. Just make sure you get everything straight again tomorrow.*

"Oh, leave me alone with all your moral lectures," I said grumpily and turned over onto my side. "Mona can think herself lucky if I manage to get her such a great guy!"

And I had secretly begun already to feel sorry that I'd written in her name rather than in my own. Perhaps Meik wasn't my ultimate dream guy, and this brilliant

---

circumstance – Umstand;
application – *hier:* Anwendung, Programm;
churned up – aufgewühlt; to grouch – meckern

Basti was! I **chased away** the thought. What kind of awful girl was I, and where would it get me?

Not into heaven, at any rate, said the grumpy voice in my inner ear.

Oh well, I didn't want to go there for the time being anyway.

The next morning I went to school feeling guilty, and avoided Mona as much as possible. Of course she noticed.

"You don't still think there's any truth to Gracia's lies?" she finally asked me directly.

"No, no, of course not," I stammered, taken by surprise, and just thought: thank goodness she knows nothing about *my* lies. I really must have been **off my rocker** yesterday.

Yet again, I couldn't follow the lesson at all.

It was particularly Wolfie's confused picture on the blackboard that **posed a conundrum to** me. And it evidently wasn't just me. Fabian put his hand up. "Herr Wolf, will this come up in the test?" he asked.

Whereupon Mona muttered to the class, "How can it come up when he doesn't get it either?"

I was so shocked by her **cheek** that I had evidently forgotten that I still had my hand up. For Wolfie came over to me and said, "What did you want to say, Kiki?"

---

to chase away – verjagen;
to be off one's rocker – übergeschnappt sein;
to pose a conundrum to sb – jmdm. ein Rätsel aufgeben;
cheek – Frechheit

"Erm, erm, I've forgotten."

"Oh, that's a shame; you're like my grandmother."

How embarrassing. At least Gracia distracted him from me.

"Herr Wolf, I didn't understand it either …"

Mona cast a pleading look up to the ceiling and cried theatrically, "Oh God, give me brains!"

There was a general **guffawing** which was by now visibly irritating Wolfie, so much so that he took a leaf out of Frau Biedermann's punishment book. "For every word more that comes from this class, the lesson will be increased by one minute."

Mona grinned. "And if we don't say anything else, can we leave earlier?"

Wolfie sighed resignedly. "I would sometimes prefer it if you weren't in my class, Ramona, erm, Marona, erm, I mean Mona."

In English with Frau Ingrimm, things got even worse, and I even got a **warning**. So I was quite relieved when the first free period came and we could go and see call-me-Uschi to choose some kissing songs for our revue. Uschi was a real **ray of sunshine**. She also **had** everything **off pat** and could immediately play all **conceivable** songs on the piano.

---

guffawing – Gelächter; warning – Verwarnung;
ray of sunshine – Lichtblick;
to have sth off pat – etwas in und auswendig kennen;
conceivable – denkbar

Singing and choosing the songs then gave us a good laugh.

Kisses under the rainbow, they bring happiness …

It was soon clear that we had to include *Kissing Forbidden* by Die Prinzen come what may. Mona was to play the role of Frau Biedermann for it. Of course we had to adapt the **lyrics** somewhat, but the chorus was already mega-suitable, and we killed ourselves laughing when Mona sang:

"Kissing forbidden, strictly forbidden.
Nobody who's ever seen me would have believed
That kissing is banned with me!"

Of course Bastian was there with a couple of kids from his class.

How embarrassing.

At least Meik still had classes, so the **intricate manoeuvrings** of my mind weren't taking place before his eyes. The Argus eyes of my friends were quite enough. The things the Pepper Dollies had seen!

At lunch my food stuck in my throat more than once in the light of their **shrewd** powers of observation.

"Did you see the way Bastian was staring at Mona?" Franzi brought up the subject over soup.

"He never stops hanging around her," Lea remarked over the main course.

"I think he wants something from her," Greetje concluded over dessert.

---

lyrics – Liedtexte;
intricate manoeuvring – kompliziertes Manöver;
shrewd – scharfsinnig

In short, the conversation over the meal **revolved** entirely **around** Mona and Bastian. What kind of **avalanche** had I started?!

So I was quite pleased when Meik came across to our table later on and asked if I wanted to go for a hot chocolate with him. I'd have done anything to get away from the Pepper Dollies. But barely had we slurped the cream off our hot chocolate before he was asking, too, "Hey, have you noticed that Bastian is interested in Mona?"

"No, I hadn't noticed," I said and couldn't help my tone of voice being slightly sour. Yet I should be glad that my strategy seemed to be working so quickly.

"But anyone can see that Bastian can't take his eyes off her, and he's always crawling around her. He even asked me if I'd **swap** roles with him."

"Which one?"

"*Gone with the Wind*. Rhett Butler."

"Well? Are you going to do it?"

"Oh, I don't know …" He gave me a **challenging** look. "Does it bother you, seeing Mona in my arms?"

"No, of course not," I immediately played it down.

"You really don't need to be jealous," said Meik with a grin.

"Me, jealous? Rubbish! I'm not jealous!"

"That's fine, then."

---

to revolve around – sich drehen um;
avalanche – Lawine;
to swap – tauschen; challenging – herausfordernd

When I got home from school that afternoon, the house was full. Dad had a load of **party** friends there, and was thinking up election campaign strategies with them.

"Oh yes, before I forget," he called to me on his way out. "If you see your boyfriend this evening ... what's his name again? ... Oh yes, Meik ... could you tell Meik, please, that he can collect the leaflets from the party office on Wednesday. And **give him my regards**."

"Eh?"

Meik, leaflets, party office? Had I missed something? I feared the worst.

So when Dad's people had gone, I asked **cautiously**, "What are the leaflets that you were talking about earlier?"

"The ones for the big **rally** in the market place."

I still didn't get it – or didn't want to get it. "What's Meik got to do with it?"

My father looked at me as if he were dealing with an idiot. "What do you mean, what's he got to do with it? He's handing them out, what else?"

I must have a hearing problem. "You mean ..." I asked again just to make sure, "you mean, Meik's supposed to do election propaganda for you?"

It must have sounded as if I were just about to spit out a completely **inedible** meal, because Dad looked at me with a frown. "Yes, of course. He's a member of our youth election team, after all. Is that a problem?"

---

party – Partei; to give sb one's regards – jmdn. grüßen; cautious – vorsichtig; rally – *hier:* Wahlkundgebung; inedible – ungenießbar

What kind of question was that? Of course it was a problem! A huge problem! I really hated it when Dad took advantage of my friends for his politics. There were **plenty of** other people who could hand out leaflets for him – party members, bored housewives, Joker. It didn't have to be my boyfriend of all people. "You should have stopped him!"

"Why? I don't see why you're so **worked up**. It's nice if one of your friends is behind my policies and supports me. I think it's really great!

Really great! Anger **rose** within me. Dad should at least keep out of my private life.

And so far as Meik was concerned, I felt deceived by him, too. Why hadn't he said anything to me about it? Hadn't I told him that I couldn't **bear** that? I didn't want a boyfriend who went electioneering for Dad. I wanted my boyfriend to be mine, all mine, and I didn't want to share him with any other girl *or* with Dad.

But there was no point arguing with Dad; when it came to arguments, he was **out of my league**. So I'd have to **settle the matter** with Meik. And so I said to my father, "I can tell him, but I wouldn't rely on Meik actually doing it."

Not if I gave him the choice between the election or me! He'd have to decide, and surely he'd prefer me, even if our relationship was in trouble at the moment.

---

plenty of – jede Menge; to be worked up – sich aufregen;
to rise – wachsen; to bear – ertragen;
to be out of one's league – nicht in der gleichen Liga spielen;
to settle the matter – eine Angelegenheit regeln

"Rubbish," replied Meik to my reproaches when we took Snuffles for a walk by the Baggersee that evening. It was unpleasantly cold and windy. The words were almost **whipped** from our mouths and blown away, all weakened. "I'm interested in politics, and that really doesn't have anything to do with you. If I hadn't gone to the rally that time, we might never have got to know one another. Who knows who you'd have tipped an ice-cream dish over!"

Did he really have to remind me of that unspeakable event? If he'd intended to **season** our conversation with humour, he'd failed to notice the seriousness of the situation.

"I hate it when my father **ropes** my friends **in** for his politics!" I said impulsively. "He **tends to devour** his helpers, you see – in terms of their time. That's why I have my principles. You have to choose: him or me!"

Meik appeared **distraught** now. His arm had been around me, protecting me from the cold wind, but now he removed it.

"I don't get you," he said, looking really unhappy as he said so. "All I want to do is support his good youth policies."

"What is there to get?" I said stroppily, "do you love me, or do you want to spend your time with my father?"

Meik looked pretty shocked then, and he **sped up** with annoyance. "Are you trying to put me to the test?

---

to whip – peitschen; to season – würzen; to rope in – einspannen; to tend to – neigen zu; to devour – verschlingen; distraught – verstört; to speed up – beschleunigen

Of course I love you, but the two things have nothing to do with one another!"

I remained grumpy and cried angrily, "They have for me! You didn't spend years suffering for your father being a prominent politician. I was invited to hundreds of children's birthday parties – not because the children wanted it, but because their mummies did! At picking-up time, they just wanted to quickly introduce the MP to all their friends: look, we **socialise with** prominent people! Oh, how I hated it! They didn't **give a toss about** me, and their stupid **brats** pulled my hair and poured hot chocolate over my best dress when their parents weren't looking!"

Meik sounded understanding as he said, "But that was ages ago. You can judge now who really likes you. After all, you've got the Pepper Dollies. So far as I'm concerned, I'm interested in politics, and it would be nice if we could hand out the leaflets for the rally together."

He sounded downright excited **at the prospect**.

At this juncture I should perhaps have just asked myself whether a little **readiness** to compromise might enable all the different interests to be **reconciled**. But no, my stubborn head had to have its way, and so I said without much thought: "No way! Decide or forget me!"

---

to socialise with – verkehren mit;
to not give a toss about sb – sich nicht um jmdn. scheren;
brat – Göre; at the prospect – bei dieser Aussicht;
at this juncture – in diesem Moment; readiness – Bereitschaft;
to reconcile – unter einen Hut bringen

Meik was silent all the way to the bus stop. Snuffles seemed to notice the bad atmosphere and ran anxiously between us, **whimpering**. Okay, I thought, so he can **agonise** a bit over his decision. The main thing is that he makes the right one. As we got to the bus stop I looked at him expectantly.

The bus came and Meik pressed a **tender** kiss into my hair, but then said, "I gave your father my word and I can't disappoint him. Sleep on it all again and remember that I love you."

Then he got into the bus. The door closed. The bus drove off.

Was that a clear decision? No!

I hated men – all of them! Regardless of whether they were boyfriends or fathers. They were a complete **error of judgement** on the part of creation!

Although Dad would no doubt rather have chilled out, he took on his children's concerns over supper. And so, to my frustration, I had to stick it out at the supper table, although I'd rather have **retreated** straight into my room.

What's more, Dad found the developments at school nowhere near as dramatic as we did. "Pretty much all European countries have school uniforms. It's time we conformed. And up to a certain age, pupils in most countries wear shorts. But maybe they'll come up with something else."

---

to whimper – winseln; to agonise – sich quälen; tender – zärtlich; error of judgement – Irrtum; to retreat – sich zurückziehen

"Well, let's hope so," said Joker, disappointed as he'd presumably expected some **decree** from his father. "If not, I'll run away with my mates."

"And so far as this kissing ban is concerned," Dad now turned his attention to the main problem, "well, it may be a somewhat unusual measure, but why not? School is for learning things, not for flirting and **smooching**. You get plenty of opportunity for that in your free time."

"You're forgetting that our school **lasts** all day. A lot of our free time takes place at school," I said, **alerting** my father **to** a not unimportant fact.

"Oh nonsense, you've still got plenty of time to spend together after school. Your new headmistress seems to be a courageous woman. We could do with more like her to head our schools!"

Slap! Well, that was one **verbal box on the ear** that I'd got. My own father was stabbing me in the back.

So was that family solidarity? My hopes were totally dashed. "And I thought you were keen on human rights."

Dad did in fact manage a grin. "There aren't any human rights to playground kissing!"

Now Mum joined in. "You don't take the children seriously," she criticised. "It's not about playground kissing for them, but a matter of principle."

---

decree – *hier:* Machtwort;
smooching – Schmusen; to last – dauern;
to alert sb to sth – *hier:* jmdn. auf etwas aufmerksam machen;
verbal box on the ear – verbale Ohrfeige

Aha, I hadn't actually seen it like that yet.

"If she's banning kissing today, then it'll be holding hands tomorrow, then flirting the day after tomorrow and …"

"Exactly," I interrupted, "and in the end, she'll ban talking, and we'll have to wear **muzzles**!"

But Dad didn't want to enter into the debate properly.

He presumably felt that he'd fulfilled his **parental** role **sufficiently**, and stood up in order to go back to his desk. "Let me know if it gets to that stage. Then I'll see what I can do for you." And to Mum he said, "I've got an important session in Berlin tomorrow morning. I'll have to get the five a.m. train."

As so often, I wished I had a father who went off to a normal office in the mornings to draw up **balance sheets** or plan production processes. Why on earth did my father's business have to be called Germany?

He gave me a quick squeeze. "Sorry, Kiki, but you'll sort it out."

Why did you have parents who had been there and done that and knew all the tricks if they simply didn't have time for their children's problems?

"I'm serious," said Joker, as he trudged off to his room. "If I have to wear short trousers, I'm pushing off."

"Will you take me with you?" I asked, completely depressed.

---

muzzle – Maulkorb; parental – elterlich; sufficient – genügend; balance sheet – Bilanz

He grinned. "'Course I will, even though you *are* a girl!"

When I had my evening goodnight phone call with Franzi, the next shock was awaiting me.

Franzi was in love. It was clear now that she was completely nuts about Raffi, that red-eared ridiculous creature. Of all people! When he **slouched** across the playground in his floppy trousers that hung so low down on his **bum** that the **crotch** was dangling around his knees, he always reminded me of a half-finished Manga figure.

But it shouldn't matter to me who Franzi took to her heart so long as there was still a bit of room in her head for me. However, it looked **dismal** on that front this evening. At any rate, her brain seemed to be completely **befuddled**. Where once my problems had been in the best hands with her, she was suddenly a complete dead loss as an agony aunt. Yes, I had the feeling that she wasn't really interested in my urgent issues any longer. Instead, she annoyed me with her own problems. My goodness, was it possible that I'd carried on just like this at the start of my relationship with Meik?

Okay, okay! Going around with your head in a pink cloud does **make** your **perception** considerably **murky**. The **threads** of my patience were slowly beginning to

---

to slouch – latschen; bum – Hintern; crotch – Schritt;
dismal – düster; befuddled – *hier:* vernebelt;
to make sth murky – etwas trüben; perception – Wahrnehmung;
thread – Faden

unravel. After all, I was pretty stressed myself after my row with Meik.

"If Raffi looks at me properly, he'll leave me then and there," Franzi whined thoughtlessly. "What with all my **spots**!"

A concluding word was **due** on my part. "My dear Franzi," I began. "You disappoint me, because your logic doesn't work. You ought to know that love is blind, and that means that so long as Raffi loves you, he can't see your spots. So if he ever starts to **fuss about** them, then something's gone wrong with his love." Bingo!

"Do you really think so?"

"Yes, really! And now a different subject: who do you think Meik loves more – my father or me?"

Silence from the other end.

"But you're not serious, are you?"

"Why not?"

"Well, that's such a **weird** question!"

"Will you have a think about it all the same? You can give me your answer tomorrow morning."

So the conversation that evening was anything but productive from my point of view.

I'd barely hung up, frustrated, when my mobile **tinkled** and announced a new text. No doubt the text was from Meik, but the **predictive texting** must have been playing tricks on him. Otherwise what he'd sent was a complete load of nonsense.

---

to unravel – auftrennen; spot – Pickel; to be due – fällig sein;
to fuss about – sich aufregen über; weird – seltsam;
to tinkle – klingeln; predictive texting – Worterkennung

I texted three question marks back to him.

Beep, beep, beep … I love my mobile.

Oh, sorry!, he wrote back.

Here's the whole thing again:

You are my happiness, you are my star,

I love you even if you're crazy!

Meik

Hahaha! So the world's laughing again! Well, I'd normally have laughed about it, but now I just felt that he wasn't taking me seriously. And that couldn't remotely be the basis for a relationship. So I decided not to communicate with him any longer until he'd given me a straight answer to my question. So there we go!

I didn't sleep well that night.

They were both lying in the hay, hurray!

Somehow, these turbulent events had driven normal school life right out of my mind. So I was completely **stunned** when Wolfie said during the next form period, "So I'll see you tomorrow at the station at seven a.m. Be on time, please."

I hadn't understood a single word he'd said, so I stared at him **blankly** and evidently inspiring pity.

"Is something not clear, Kiki?"

Erm, yes, you could say that – everything, to be precise.

"Station?" I asked hesitantly.

But before Wolfie could answer me, Franzi did it for him. "Class trip! Is the penny beginning to drop?"

Hmm, yes, the penny was beginning to drop. Oh horrors. Not that terrible sporty canoeing trip to the **'hay-hotel'**? That wasn't supposed to take place until the end of May.

---

hay – Heu; to be stunned – fassungslos sein;
blank – verständnislos; hay-hotel – Hotel im Heu

"It is the end of May," said Franzi drily.

My goodness, so it was, where had all that time gone? Somehow life seemed to dash past me at top speed.

"Don't forget to pack your rain-gear, it might get a bit wet. The weather forecast isn't that good."

Oh great. Wet on top, wet below – I just loved sailing in the rain.

"By the way, two pupils are coming with us who are in a position of trust. Meik and Mariam from Year Nine."

Wow! I couldn't believe it! Oh, thank you, thank you, fate! Now it could rain cats and dogs; if Meik were there, the sun would be shining everywhere for me! At any rate, if he answered my question and **ditched** his stupid politics for me. But I was in fact thoroughly convinced that he would do so.

Wolfie was **hum-ing and haw-ing** about something else. Somehow he seemed not to be able to spit it out.

"Is there something else, Herr Wolf?" I tried to help him on his way.

"Yes, there is," he said quietly. "There's just one more small matter. Frau Springer, your sport teacher, is unfortunately not very well – a **slipped disc**. There's no way she can come ..."

"Oh, what a shame, but it's not that bad either ..." Mona interrupted **consolingly**.

"... as a substitute," he said, "Frau Biedermann would love to come!"

---

to ditch – sausen lassen; to hum and haw – herumdrucksen; slipped disc – Bandscheibenvorfall; consoling – tröstend

A bursting stink-bomb couldn't have created more horror than this announcement.

"She – she's a keen canoeist …" Wolfie tried to **justify** our headmistress's completely frightful request.

I couldn't believe it! Naturally, complete chaos **erupted**, and practically everyone wanted to drop out of the trip. But Wolfie somehow managed to talk us out of it. He reminded us of the cost and of how long we'd spent preparing for it. The 'hay-hotel' and the train tickets were already reserved, the food for the barbecue had already been bought … and, and, and! By the time the lesson ended, our nerves couldn't take any more either. Wolfie had gone on at us **to such an extent** that we finally gave in.

"But if she comes out with her kissing ban on the trip, too, then I'll make sure she **capsizes**," hissed Fabian.

"Oh my goodness," groaned Greetje at break, and I said, completely frustrated, "What have we done to **deserve** this?"

"We don't deserve it," said Franzi. "We're getting it for nothing. That's precisely the problem. You can't return presents, you see."

"Great present," muttered Lea. "Did you see the way

---

to justify – rechtfertigen;
to erupt – ausbrechen;
to such an extent – in solchem Ausmaß;
to capsize – kentern;
to deserve – verdienen

Gracia was grinning? She's bound to spend the whole trip **sucking up to** the headmistress!"

"Shame on you," said Greetje, giving me a friendly **reproof**, "don't say such things!"

"Better not to do such things!" countered Lea.

Franzi, however, was optimistic and reckoned that the trip would be pretty cool, and she said to me, "How did you **wangle** that – getting Meik to come?"

I didn't, I thought, but if she thought I was capable of that, then I was quite happy to let her believe it. "Ah well, I have my connections!" I replied.

Unfortunately, I had to leave my circle of friends early and collect the brush from the caretaker so I could sweep the playground. At least I met Meik there. He took the bin and the **shovel** and so we got down to our **communal** cleaning job as the bell rang.

Of course I immediately asked him about the canoeing trip. "So how come you of all people is coming with us?"

It turned out that Meik had been in the canoe club since Year Five, and almost always accompanied class trips as a tutor. "When I heard that you were going this weekend, of course I immediately **volunteered**. A weekend with you in the 'hay-hotel' sounds fantastic."

"A weekend with me and Biedermann," I dampened his enthusiasm.

But he already knew about that, and remained opti-

---

to suck up to sb – jmdm. in den Hintern kriechen; reproof – Rüge; to wangle – drehen; shovel – Schaufel; communal – Kommunal-; to volunteer – sich freiwillig melden

mistic. "Oh, I don't think it's that **grim**; we'll get her out of the way somehow."

Okay, I thought, so it might be quite nice. There was just one **teeny-weeny** problem. And so I put the modified Gretchen question to him with a faintly ironic smile, "Erm, by the way, before I forget – what are you doing about me and politics?"

Meik leaned on the brush and looked uncomfortably at me. "Is it really that important to you?"

True: I was wondering exactly the same in view of the imminent class trip we were going on together, but at the end of the day, I had my principles. "Yes, it is. I don't like you doing election campaigning for my father."

His face turned sad and I looked away. "This really isn't the right place to discuss it," he said.

"Oh yes, it is! I think this is a very suitable place. Quite sufficient for a short answer."

"But it can't be dealt with with a simple yes or no. There's just too much hanging on it for both of us."

I became suspicious. That didn't look like a clear decision **in my favour**. Now spit it out, boy, I thought. Even bad news has to be passed on at some point. Then again, no … maybe better to wait until after the canoeing trip? But then I wouldn't get a single peaceful minute. No, he had to decide immediately, here and now. "So, what's it going to be? My father or me?"

He **squirmed** visibly. "But Kiki, listen, you mean a lot to me, but so does my political work …"

---

grim – schlimm; teeny-weeny – winzig;
in one's favour – zu jmds. Gunsten; to squirm – sich winden

"You can't have both! Not with me! Not with my father!"

"Why on earth not? To be honest, I just don't understand you …"

"I've noticed." I reached angrily for the rubbish bin and dragged it behind me in the direction of the caretaker.

Meik ran alongside me. "Just wait. I … oh … why are you making it so difficult for us?"

"You're making it difficult, not me."

"I can't go back on my word because …"

I stopped abruptly and looked him in the face. "You're not serious?" I snapped at him.

"There must be some compromise …"

"No! I hate poor compromises and I hate you!" With these words I turned and ran into the school.

He really mustn't see my tears!

Of course this argument hugely **diminished** my pleasure at the prospect of the class trip. I was even close to phoning in sick.

But then Franzi rang and was so bubbling over with get-up-and-go that I somehow didn't see why I should let Meik **spoil** the whole fun of it. Maybe he'd think better of it on the class trip. I wanted to give us the chance, at any rate. So in the afternoon I started to feel very excited about the journey.

"Has anyone seen my raincoat?" I cried throughout the house.

---

to diminish – dämpfen; to spoil – verderben

The only one who could hear my question was Joker, and he was a **notorious hoarder** and never-find-it-again type. I couldn't expect any real help from him, even if he did roll off the sofa and offer to help me to look.

"And my joggers are in the wash," I grumbled on.

"Didn't you know that you were going on this trip tomorrow?" asked my brother.

"Yes, I did know, actually, but I'd totally forgotten. No wonder, with all this stress that Biedermann's created. Oh, by the way, she's coming with us ..."

My brother gave me a look of deepest sympathy. "Hey, if you want to be ill ... I've got a great trick with the thermometer ..."

I shook my head and pulled the missing raincoat out from under the Pop Sofa. "That's very kind, but I can't **leave** my friends **in the lurch**, and in any case, Meik's going, too."

Joker, still unaware of the most recent crisis in our relationship, gave me a meaningful look. "Well, Mum will be quite pleased that Biedermann is going, too."

She was indeed. As if I didn't know what was right and what wasn't! But Mum must somehow connect hay with rather **dodgy** thoughts of her youth, so she was extremely suspicious. The knowledge that Frau Biedermann was accompanying us evidently reassured her greatly.

When everything was packed, I sat down at the PC

---

notorious – berühmt-berüchtigt; hoarder – Sammler;
to leave sb in the lurch – jmdn. im Stich lassen;
dodgy – fragwürdig;

once more. I wanted to have a quick look and see if there was perhaps an e-mail for M-lieschen.

And in fact, three unread e-mails popped up in the inbox.

Three??? Well, Bastian was rather overdoing it.

Two of the e-mails, however, soon turned out to be adverts for mobile ring-tones and a book-club. But the third one was indeed from him.

It was a greetings card depicting a heavily **laden** hay-wagon. **Underneath**, it said simply but sweetly:

*Have fun in the hay – and be **faithful** to me!*

My goodness, he was going for it. Really taking possession good and proper.

What would Mona reply to that one? Something clever, no doubt. I pondered for a while, but as I wasn't feeling very creative after all my frustrations with Meik, I came up only with a rather normal solution. I decided on an animated card with a butterfly flying onto a flower. Then I wrote:

I'm a bright butterfly, I fly here and there ...

It was a line from an old pop song about passionate love, **fidelity** and little affairs that Mum often played on the piano. A gentle **rebuff** through the flowers, which Mona would probably have given with a **wink**, too. Motto: not so fast, my dear! There are other people I could be sniffing around!

The e-mail was sent again. From M-lieschen to Bastinochild, and I hoped that it would make Mona

---

laden – beladen; underneath – darunter; faithful – treu; fidelity – Treue; rebuff – Abfuhr; wink – Augenzwinkern

even more interesting to Bastian. Precisely because my relationship with Meik was in crisis, it was important to take her out of circulation.

Pretty much half-asleep, I boarded the train the next morning. Mum had driven me to the station and had given me a couple of **tasty treats** in addition to the usual warnings. I got stuck into them with the Pepper Dollies the minute we'd occupied our compartment.

Of course it **enticed** unwanted guests. Fabian, Sebastian and Raffi stormed our compartment and we could only get rid of them by buying our freedom with a bag of Crunchips.

From the station, a chartered bus ran to a **ramblers'** car park on the moors, from where we reached the **jetty** after a 15-minute walk. Already awaiting us were the boats which the canoe club had dropped off the day before. From here, we were supposed to go to the 'hay-hotel' and then back to school the following day; the school had its own landing stage at the **edge** of the river. This meant that canoeing had played a similarly large role at our school as in Cambridge for example.

It was damp, as a fine **drizzle** of the kind that **penetrated** everything was falling from the icy grey sky. The mood was **correspondingly** dampened.

What's more, I had the feeling that I had Frau Bie-

---

tasty treat – Leckerei; to entice – anlocken;
rambler – Wanderer/Wanderin; jetty – Anlegesteg;
edge – Rand, Ufer; drizzle – Nieselregen;
to penetrate – durchdringen; corresponding – entsprechend

dermann's gaze constantly boring into my neck, which meant that I kept **manically** turning round when I was trying to get the boat ready.

"My God," said Franzi, rather annoyed. "Have you got some kind of **persecution complex** today?"

I pulled myself together and was finally sitting in the same boat as Franzi and the Pepper Dollies.

"You look as if you can manage on your own," Frau Biedermann remarked and chose the rather **gormless**-seeming Slugs for herself. Well, Gracia would be able to get stuck straight into some serious sucking-up. Wolfie decided to **entrust** Fabian and the Gorillas to Meik, and to row with the rather more gentle types like little Raffi himself. Mariam took pity on the remaining girls. Then we cast off with five boats. At first the journey was pretty **cosy**; the river, not seven metres wide, snaked in gentle bends through **meadows**, fields and woods. Then we had to cross a long thin lake.

"Look, water lilies," said Greetje in delight, and in front of us Fabian held his arm in the water to catch a fat **carp**. Which was not in fact successful, but did, however, almost capsize the boat.

Then it turned difficult as we had to get over a **weir**. Basically it was no big deal, though, as the slight difference in levels was easily **circumvented** by going down a **slipway**. You just had to take your courage in both

---

manic – manisch; persecution complex – Verfolgungswahn;
gormless – dämlich; to entrust – anvertrauen; cosy – gemütlich;
meadow – Wiese; carp – Karpfen; weir – Wehr;
to circumvent – umgehen; slipway – Bootsrutsche

hands and let yourself slide down into the water which, it's true, was more turbulent. We'd already managed it and were rocking gently in calmer waters again when we suddenly saw a boat lying diagonally in the water and being carried right across to the little waterfall at the edge of the weir.

"Oh my God, what are they doing there?" Lea screamed. Something seemed to be very wrong.

Daphne and Gracia were waving their **oars** around wildly in the air whilst Frau Biedermann and Lydia were in the **bow**, desperately trying to steer the boat in a different direction.

"Left," Frau Biedermann was yelling. "Stick the left oar in and row against the **current** ..."

But that seemed not to work either. Suddenly the front of Meik's boat appeared in the background and at that moment a rope flew across to Frau Biedermann. She caught it and pressed it into Gracia's hand.

"Hold on to it and don't let go," she commanded.

Rowing hard, Meik and the Gorillas managed to drag the Slugs' boat round. For one short moment the **stern** and the screaming Daphne hung in the air above the **precipice** of the weir, but then the boat slowly moved against the current back into the middle of the river. The dangerous situation was under control. We breathed a sigh of relief when everyone had finally **negotiated** the weir.

Even Frau Biedermann looked a bit pale around the

---

oar – Ruder; bow – Bug; current – Strömung; stern – Heck; precipice – Abgrund; to negotiate – *hier:* überwinden nose. Only Wolfie, whose boat was miles behind everybody else's, hadn't seen any of the drama. And when he suddenly appeared at the edge of the weir and his boat took off as if it were ski-jumping, we all let out a cry, although basically nothing could surprise us now. The boat sailed about two metres through the air like an airship, then splashed into the water right in front of us with such a **jerk** that some of its human **cargo** tipped overboard with a multi-voiced yell. The sinking of the Titanic had nothing on the drama that now happened around Wolfie's boat. Everyone was splashing and shouting and outdoing one another to get involved in a rescue operation. Whilst Wolfie was pulled from the waters by Frau Biedermann in person, Franzi grabbed Raffi by the collar and pulled him into our boat.

"Hey, are you trying to capsize us?" I snapped at her as the boat began to overbalance.

"I can't let him **drown**, for heaven's sake," **retorted** Franzi, and everything was in fact fine. We rowed carefully to the shore and not long afterwards the rest of Wolfie's team **moored** their boat and took their **dripping** crew members back on board.

The journey could continue.

Somewhat **whacked**, we finally reached our destination. My hands were damp and icy cold, and I could barely hold my oar. I could hardly feel my feet in my wet trainers. Sport is murder, let me tell you!

---

jerk – Ruck; cargo – Fracht;
to drown – ertrinken; to retort – zurückschnauzen;
to moor – vertäuen; dripping – triefend; whacked – kaputt

We moored the boats at the jetty and **clambered** onto dry land. A few metres away, at the edge of the forest, was a **lowly** building with a roof of straw. Our 'hay-hotel'!

"Hay" was right, but "hotel" was rather an exaggeration for this former sheep-**pen** which had had a couple of loads of hay tipped onto its **clay** floor. For there was no room at the inn, I thought. This must be pretty similar to what Mary and Joseph encountered in their day. In short: wretchedly rustic.

"Are we supposed to sleep on the floor?" Gracia immediately **scoffed**. She screwed up her nose. Whether it was because of the **accommodation** or because of the intense stink of hay wasn't quite clear.

Daphne and Lydia were also standing, rather at a loss, in the entrance. Admittedly, we were all a bit shocked. We hadn't imagined that this whole thing would be quite so in touch with nature.

"Birkenstock!" Franzi hissed to me. "It's his fault; he **tipped** Wolfie **off**."

Then it was all clear. This must be where he spent his alternative summer holidays **knitting** muesli socks out of sheep's wool.

The **sheepfold** consisted of two differently-sized rooms which were separated by a narrow corridor. You could see the larger room above a low wall. Both rooms

---

to clamber – klettern; lowly – bescheiden, schlicht; pen – Stall; clay – Lehm; to scoff – spotten; accommodation – Unterbringung; to tip sb off – jmdm. einen Tipp geben; to knit – stricken; sheepfold – Schafstall

could be shut from the outside with iron gates. Like in the zoo, I thought, and could well imagine the Gorillas behind the bars of the gate.

They did in fact feel right at home. Fabian and his men stormed into the big room howling loudly, threw their rucksacks and sleeping bags down into the empty feed-**troughs**, and began a good hay-fight. It was only logical for us girls to slip off into the smaller room to make it all a bit more homely.

At least Wolfie and Frau Biedermann didn't intend to sleep in the **stable** as well. They were instead housed in a caravan that stood a short distance away from the stable. That was at least one ray of hope. However, whether Frau Biedermann would start by **drying** Wolfie **off** remained a mystery to us, unfortunately enough. But the pair of them had evidently got a bit closer, because when they reappeared they didn't just seem refreshed but also not so grumpy as at school.

Nevertheless, Frau Biedermann immediately started giving orders again. Wasn't it enough for her to take care of our Wolfie, who was evidently not fit for life? "I'm relying on you to follow your tutors' orders. They're acting on our instructions. Do you hear? You must at all costs – and I repeat: *at all costs* – **obey** their orders. Anyone who doesn't do as they're told will be sent home!"

It was agreed that Meik would sleep with the boys and Mariam with the girls, and that everyone was to settle down for the night at ten-thirty.

---

trough – Trog; stable – Stall;
to dry sb off – *hier:* jmdn. trockenlegen; to obey – gehorchen

We **lugged** the rest of our bags and the provisions round. A **patio** under a huge lime-tree was chosen and partly covered over. A large barbecue area raised our hopes of a tasty meal.

Firstly, however, we wanted to rid ourselves of our damp clothes and deal with a couple of other bodily needs.

"Is there a loo anywhere?" asked Franzi. "Or are we supposed to go in the **undergrowth**?"

Not exactly, but almost. There was a loo, but it was dead ecological, as the smell told us from miles off.

"Yuck! A hole in the ground! How unhygienic!" raged Daphne. "And full of flies! I'm not using that!"

Then your bladder's going to burst, I thought unsympathetically, although I didn't find it exactly great either. At least there were separate cubicles for boys and girls. On the door of the boys' loo was a poster with a guy from a comic with his trousers down who was just making a **cascading arch** in the air. Underneath it said: *Please wee sitting down!*

Naturally, this gave rise to a couple of dirty remarks. But taking everything together, it was better than **squatting on the bog** with a naked backside out there in the rain.

When we then tried to put our dry clothes on, it all started. My goodness, did the Gorillas ever have a lot of hormones!

---

to lug – schleppen; patio – Innenhof;
undergrowth – Gestrüpp; cascading arch – hoher Bogen;
to squat on the bog – *hier:* auf dem Donnerbalken hocken

"Heeeeey, Kiki, hot bum!" bawled Fabian, who was standing in the open doorway with his legs apart. Whereupon Greetje pulled the iron gate shut and hung a blanket over it.

"**Spoil-sport**!"

Gracia suddenly squealed loudly. As if she'd been bitten by a tarantula. Not a tarantula, exactly, but it was a spider. She whirled around like a **dervish**, hopping from one leg to the other.

It was a mega-fat **hunter spider** with disgusting hairy legs that had given her such a shock. I had nothing against spiders, which are actually very useful because they devour all sorts of insects. But the thought that there were evidently all kinds of creatures here as food for these fat spiders wasn't quite so great.

"What sorts of things live in hay?" I asked Franzi.

"Erm, I've never thought about it. Just little creatures. **Mites**, **aphids**, spiders, grasshoppers, beetles, **ticks** ..."

"Stop it," I said, and the desire to throw ourselves spontaneously into the hay as the boys had done just didn't so much as appear.

But when Meik and Wolfie then lit the barbecue and we were all huddled under the protective **canopy** staring into the fire with the smell of sausages wafting around our noses, we were to some extent reconciled to our surroundings after all. I stole a glance across at Meik, but when our eyes met I quickly looked away.

---

spoil-sport – Spielverderber; dervish – Derwisch;
hunter spider – Jagdspinne; mite – Milbe; aphid – Blattlaus;
tick – Zecke; canopy – Vordach

Frau Biedermann appeared distinctly peaceable and spent pretty much the whole time going on at Wolfie, who even laughed at something or another every now and then. She was wearing sporty jeans and a washed-out hooded sweatshirt bearing the logo of a canoe club which she evidently belonged to. With no make-up on, she had **freckles** on her nose and the sharp, ascetic **features** of an extreme sportswoman.

She seemed to be completely programmed for high achievement. Strange, then, that she **derived pleasure from** Wolfie. Ah well, they were pretty close spiritually speaking. Only she was a lot more capable of getting things done, which no doubt impressed Wolfie **beyond all measure**. At any rate, his puppy-dog eyes were fixed on his "rescuer" for the entire evening.

"Good arm muscles," remarked Franzi.

I looked at my pale, thin and painful upper arms. Maybe I should actually do a bit more for my fitness levels and transform my idea of doing more with the canoe club into reality. Canoeing was actually a very enjoyable sport, especially when Meik was in the canoeing club! Oh, things could have been so lovely for us. Why was it so complicated all of a sudden?

I cast a look across to him as I thought this, and just saw Mona planting herself next to him by the fire. She was wearing the **scruffiest** gear possible: a baggy sweatshirt and washed-out leggings, and yet every boy was

---

freckle – Sommersprosse; features – *hier:* Gesichtszüge;
to derive pleasure from – Gefallen finden an;
beyond all measure – über alle Maßen; scruffy – vergammelt

scurrying around after her, covering her with **daisies**, making her **dandelion** chains or bringing her sausages, salad or something to drink. She laughed **incessantly** and did appear to be enjoying the trip enormously.

How could someone be so positive in any kind of situation? I didn't get it. She really was a class above me there. I just let **adverse** circumstances bring me down too quickly. Far too little self-confidence. Unfounded **inferiority** complex, Franzi called it. Okay, if I put my mind to it, no doubt I'd be able to wrap a bunch of boys around my little finger, too. Fabian, for example, or Sebastian. But did I want to? No! Meik was enough for me. However, he should jolly well be there just for me, too. With heart and mind!

Of course Mona infected everyone with her cheerfulness and desire for action. And when we went to see the sheep in the field after we'd eaten, she was the first one to try to ride one of the two **donkeys** in a neighbouring field. True, she didn't even manage to **mount** it, but the Gorillas immediately copied her.

Fabian was stupid enough to jump onto the poor creature in wild-west style. Barely had he landed on its back when it tried with wild **bucks** to throw him off again. He did cling heroically to its **mane**, but finally landed in a pile of **squelchy** mud that the donkeys'

---

to scurry around – herumhuschen; daisy – Gänseblümchen; dandelion – Löwenzahn; incessant – unablässig; adverse – widrig; inferiority – Minderwertigkeit; donkey – Esel; to mount – aufsteigen; buck – Bocksprung; mane – Mähne; squelchy – *hier:* weich

hooves had made in the field. This made him rather muddy, but on the other hand, he didn't break his **coccyx** when he landed rather un-gently on his backside.

"Maybe you should try a real horse rather than a donkey!" said Greetje, giggling as she alluded to *Manitu's Shoe*.

It was great fun, and every guy, Meik included, now of course had to prove how **gutsy** he was. Hard as nails! As most of the girls didn't dare to ride the donkeys, someone came up with the idea of trying our hands at riding the sheep, until Biedermann got wind of what was going on and forbade us any further cowboy games. Before the **German Heath Sheep** set about us with their horns, thank God. But it really was quite an experience, feeling a fat, woolly sheep under your bum, and dashing out in the wilds clinging on to its **shaggy** fleece! Seriously groovy, to put it in my brother's slang.

"Did you really take a photo of me?" I asked Greetje after surviving the ride intact.

"Of course, at precisely the moment that your sheep shot off like a rocket!"

"I absolutely have to have a copy for my brother," I demanded. "Or else he'll never believe me!"

When we returned, exhausted and filthy, Frau Biedermann and Mariam had made a huge pot of chilli con carne, and as we spooned the hot **brew** into ourselves, we almost felt like real gauchos.

---

coccyx – Steißbein; gutsy – mutig;
German Heath Sheep – Heidschnucke; shaggy – zottelig
brew – Gebräu

At **twilight**, garden torches were driven into the ground and we sang songs. However, when Mona started to sing *Kissing Forbidden*, the rehearsal of which was supposed to be a secret, the mood abruptly changed. Wolfie and Frau Biedermann stood up.

"Time for bed," said the headmistress, visibly **peeved**. "And go to sleep, please. We want to row off in good time tomorrow morning."

Wolfie extinguished the torches and the fire with her, and then the pair of them disappeared into their caravan.

Fabian made ape noises as they went. "Hope it all turns out okay. Hope our Wolfie doesn't turn into a wolf!"

"You'd better watch yourself or you'll turn into an ape," Meik advised him drily.

After a certain **decent** interval during which we waited to see if Frau Biedermann would do another tour of inspection – which she did – the clear **gender divide** was suddenly **abolished**. Whilst the Slugs and a couple of other boys and girls had already gone to bed in the smaller room, the midnight party began in the bigger room. The Pepper Dollies and I fetched our blankets and sleeping bags and we soon had a gigantic cosy camp.

One of the Gorillas conjured up a couple of bottles of **fig** vodka and passed them around. Brr, no thanks! Meik and Mariam squeezed their eyes shut and even took a

---

twilight – Dämmerung; peeved – eingeschnappt;
decent – angemessen; gender divide – Geschlechtertrennung;
to abolish – *hier:* aufheben; fig – Feige

swig each. Raffi, however, had had at least three or four swigs and was therefore **conspicuously** relaxed all of a sudden. This showed itself among other things by the fact that he started **pawing** Franzi at any available opportunity. But she seemed to find it all quite okay; she just giggled unnaturally shrilly every now and then when he **buried himself** in her hair and tried to kiss her neck.

"Want a couple of puffs?" Sebastian suddenly whispered to me, and held out a glowing **fag**.

But before I could refuse because I really wasn't into that whole smoking **lark**, Meik had already wrenched the cigarette from his hand. "Are you nuts!" he yelled. "Do you want to set fire to us all?" And he **bellowed** to the others: "**Woe betide anyone who** smokes here! I'll single-handedly chuck them in the river to put it out!"

Okay, so he was right, but did he have to start shouting about it?

At that moment it was really embarrassing to have him as a boyfriend, and I slid away from him, right into the Pepper Dollies' corner.

After that the good atmosphere had gone and since everyone was tired anyway, it gradually went quieter and quieter, and soon the peaceful breathing of the sleepers was all that could be heard, interrupted every now and then by the snoring of the people with

---

swig – Schluck; conspicuous – auffallend; to paw – betatschen;
to bury oneself – sich vergraben; fag – Zigarettenkippe;
lark – Jux, Fez; to bellow – brüllen;
Woe betide anyone who … – Wehe dem, der …

blocked-up noses. I was already dozing off when Meik came crawling over to me again. Was he going to make an attempt at **reconciliation**?

"Sweet dreams," I heard him whispering, and then my eyes closed.

The next morning I was awoken by the **chirruping** of birds. All my bones hurt. I sat up in a daze and looked around in confusion. Then it gradually began to dawn on me where I was. I cast a look over my classmates, who were still sleeping. Then my heart almost stopped.

Lying right next to the Gorillas was Mona. Her long, dyed-red hair was tousled, with blades of grass and daisies in its **strands**. It was half covering her face. A naked, muscular arm was lying on her sleeping bag. I'm going to **have a fit**, it flashed through my mind, and I put my hand to my mouth so as not to cry out loud. The arm on Mona's sleeping bag belonged to none other than Meik, who was lying next to Mona, half in and half out of his sleeping bag.

I'm going to kill her, I thought, I'm going to kill both of them!

But before I could do it, someone rattled violently on the iron-barred gate.

"Open up!" yelled Daphne. "Which idiot locked us in here!"

When I went over to undo the locks, a howling Gra-

---

reconciliation – Versöhnung; chirruping – Zwitschern; strand – Strähne; to have a fit – einen Anfall haben

cia also appeared and **wailed**, "I'm dying, oh, oh, oh, I'm dying!"

She did indeed look pitiful. Her whole face was swollen. Even her eyelids and lips were swollen.

Mariam had also immediately jumped out of bed and I asked her, "What's the matter with Gracia?"

"Looks like a hay-allergy," she replied, then asked Gracia if she'd ever suffered from **hay fever**.

"Not so far," the latter said, shaking her head.

Mariam grabbed her by the arm and pulled her out of the stable. "Come on, get out of here and get under the shower to get rid of the dust and **pollen** and stuff. Maybe you're allergic to mites, too."

Then she asked me, "Could you help her?"

Me? Why me? Couldn't Daphne or Lydia ... After all, I had my own problems! Oh well, fine, okay, okay, so I'd do my Mother Teresa act and I'd fly at Meik's and Mona's throats a bit later on!

It turned out that various other people were also suffering from severe hay fever attacks. Frau Biedermann immediately took over the crisis management and began organising transport via mobile for at least the most serious cases.

The rest of us left together after breakfast and continued our boat journey. Frau Biedermann stayed behind with the hay-victims and waited for their alarmed parents.

"What's up?" Franzi asked after a while. "You look very grim."

---

to wail – jammern; hay fever – Heuschnupfen; pollen – Pollen

Unlike me, she looked relaxed and chilled-out, not to say happy. What must Raffi have whispered to her yesterday in his **tipsy** state?

Should I tell her about this morning's shock? No, better not to, it was uncool. And if Franzi were to be sympathetic, I'd go all wet and **weepy**. So I just said: "Oh, it's not important. Just do me a favour. Shoot me if I ever start anything with a boy again!"

---

tipsy – beschwipst; weepy – weinerlich

Crises of the heart

At home, I threw myself on my bed first off and shut my family out of my room on the grounds that I was over-tired and **drained**.

However, Joker, with his lust for sensation, had no sympathy for that.

But Mum, who presumably still had good memories of class trip nights she'd experienced, supported me. "Let Kiki chill out a bit. You two can talk later."

I had a hot shower, disappeared back into my room with a steaming pot of vanilla tea, and locked the door. Then I sat at the PC to check my e-mails.

They included a card from Bastinochild. It was an invitation to his birthday party.

Blimey, he was going to be 17 already! Wow! That would be one fabulous party. How cool that he was inviting me!

Or … something terrible suddenly dawned on me. He didn't mean me, of course! He meant the anony-

---

drained – ausgelaugt

mous e-mailer who, to make matters worse, he must **assume** was Mona.

What on earth had I started? Now Meik *and* Bastian both fancied her! And me ... who loved me?

Fate was being so unjust again, I thought, as I logged out and closed the programme. I didn't feel in a position to answer just at the moment.

But when I was lying in bed staring at the dark ceiling, I **gradually** came to a decision. I would trick Mona and show Meik that like hell would I cry about him!

I would go to Bastian's birthday party myself. Come what may!

The telephone rang. At this hour? That was actually *my* "I've-got-an-urgent-problem" time.

I had, **thus far,** considered it completely impossible that Franzi would have such a thing because she a) always had her life under control in a single-minded and methodical kind of way, and b) she was creative and clever enough to have an immediate solution to hand if a problem arose. Unlike me.

Today, however, the GILM, the Greatest Imaginable Love Mishap, seemed to have befallen her.

"The lousy little creature!" she snapped down my ear. "The little Nothing, the little wimp!"

Oh God, what had happened? I didn't dare to ask, so furious was she.

"They'll have to scrape him off the floor if I get my hands on him again!"

---

to assume – annehmen; gradual – schrittweise; thus far – so weit

"Who?" I wanted to know exactly who she meant, although I could pretty much imagine. Only a boy could upset a girl to that extent. And with Franzi, there could only be one suspect. Too right ...

"Raffi of course, who else!"

Yes, who else indeed. Now it'd have been interesting to know the reason why Franzi had gone off at the deep end. She spat it out without being asked. **Literally**, because 'speaking' really wasn't the word for it. What she emitted sounded like a single puke-aria.

What terrible thing could the boy have done to her?

"He's left me! He dumped me, and do you know how?"

Of course I didn't know – although I did know this: dumping is dumping, and the 'how' really makes no difference. However, it evidently did make a difference, for there were apparently various levels of **vileness**, and the most **despicable** thing of all had happened to my friend Franzi.

"A text, he sent me a despicable text. Like Naddel did to Ralf Siegel! The lousy little ..."

I shut my ears, because I didn't want to hear what Raffi was in her eyes. A text really wasn't very stylish. But was it worse than seeing the naked arm of your own boyfriend on your rival's sleeping bag? I sighed self-pityingly but then asked, **feigning** interest, "So did he at least give you a reason? Why all of a sudden? Yesterday in the hay you were one heart and one soul."

---

literal – sprichwörtlich; vileness – Niedertracht;
despicable – verabscheuungswürdig; to feign – vortäuschen

Now that Franzi's initial anger had blown over, her voice sounded pretty watery, and her words were interrupted every now and then by sniffs. "That's what I thought, too ... just imagine my shock ..."

I certainly could imagine it, I could vividly imagine it and could comprehend it completely in my situation, but ... "So what's the reason, eh?"

"He writes ... no, I can't say it ... it's better if I forward his text to your mobile ..."

No sooner said than done. Moments later my mobile **purred** and I stared, perplexed, at the display.

Franzikins (oh no-oo!) *we have to split up. I love you so much, but I don't feel ready for a relationship yet.*

Forgive me,

Your loving Rafael

Rafael! Blimey, that really did sound serious. But on the other hand ...

"Do you reckon he's got someone else?" Franzi **jerked** me out of my **reverie**. "No boy leaves a girl because he loves her too much. That's sick."

Well, it's not exactly the norm, but such things do happen from time to time. Whatever. The business didn't seem as tragic as I'd initially feared. It was a question of building Franzi up and working out what could still be **salvaged**. "Well, it seems to me that he's got cold feet. But that's quite normal and doesn't have anything to do with you. It's all just immature, **adolescent** hot air. He would like to, but he doesn't dare to. Maybe he's one

---

to purr – schnurren; to jerk – reißen; reverie – Träumerei;
to salvage – retten; adolescent – pubertär

of the **tempestuous** types and he's afraid that he won't be able to keep himself under control ..."

Okay, this was rather wild speculation, especially where little Raffi was concerned. Franzi, however, would be flattered by the idea that she could drive a boy so wild that his only option was to flee. I'd calculated the effect of my words correctly.

She was already sounding considerably more optimistic when she now said, "You ... you ... think he's leaving me because he loves me too much? Because he's afraid of jumping on me?"

Hmm, so that wasn't what I directly intended to say, but okay, if she thought so ... "You just drove him completely crazy in the hay! And now he's afraid he's not in control of his feelings and ..." I said the words, "... his **urges**."

"No!"

"Yes! That's how it sometimes is with boys. As you've said so accurately yourself: they're slaves to their hormones!"

After that, there really wasn't anything to add to the topic.

And so Franzi sighed, relatively **consoled**, "The main thing is he loves me, and I'll sort everything else out."

Did that girl ever have a cheerful disposition.

Is there anything more depressing than rehearsing for a revue on kissing while you're drowning in unhappy

---

tempestuous – stürmisch; urge – Trieb; consoled – getröstet

love? I'd sooner die! I don't know either why I had to put myself through this intensified torture on Monday instead of just staying in bed. But humans are creatures of **habit**, and it was habit that made me wake up on time and dutifully set off on my way to school. Only once I was standing at the bus-stop did I fully realise what I was putting myself through. All my anger with Meik and Mona arose in me along with my breakfast egg, and I could have puked.

What on earth must have gone on between them in the hay once I'd gone to sleep? My imagination blew strange bubbles and my anger increased beyond all measure in the face of these terrible visions. At the same time, however, I felt a dull sadness about the loss of my first love. I had to face the painful fact that I'd lost Meik. He evidently preferred not only politics but also Mona to me. Of course she undoubtedly hadn't stuck a pistol to his **chest** as I did. But she didn't have an MP as a father! Sigh!

I got on the bus and stared through the dirty window panes at the houses as they flew past. There were so many unpleasant areas in our town! For a moment I wondered whether I couldn't win Meik back and whether I shouldn't fight for him. But then I saw Mona with her **radiant** smiles and her model-like aura and immediately felt distinctly average and unattractive. She was the exotic beauty and I was the girl next door! And it was obvious which the boys preferred.

---

habit – Gewohnheit; chest – Brust; radiant – strahlend

You and your inferiority complex, my inner coach said nastily. *More self-confidence, Bella! Remember Percy at the fashion show!* I had to grin at the memory. He really had tried to get off with me. But I'd looked seriously hot then, too. *And so you do now,* my inner coach encouraged me. *If you want, you could have five guys in each hand!* Hmm, yes that was in fact true. Was I supposed to join a **nunnery** on Meik's account? No way! I had no intention of doing that! After all, there were lots more boys in the world and if I thought about it properly, there were even some really sweet ones. Bastian, for example, was good-looking; he was the student head so he was no doubt not stupid, and also wrote mega-romantic e-mails. What was I thinking of, pairing off such a great guy with Mona of all people?

It couldn't be difficult to convert him back – to me, I thought! All I had to do was out myself somehow as the writer of the M-lieschen e-mails. His birthday party was bound to give me the opportunity to do so.

After all this thinking, I was already feeling a lot better. No more of this **wimpishness**! Action was called for. I would **spin** the **wheel of fortune** a bit myself, and then we'd see if I couldn't get it to swing in the right direction.

All morning I punished Meik by ignoring him. When he called to me in the cafeteria, I acted as if I hadn't heard him. Huh! He could just **stew in his own juices**.

---

nunnery – Kloster; wimpishness – Feigheit;
to spin – drehen; wheel of fortune – Schicksalsrad;
to stew in one's own juices – in seinem eigenen Saft schmoren

Of course Franzi finally noticed my strange behaviour despite her problems with Raffi.

"Why are you being so unfriendly to Meik?" she asked without **beating around the bush**. "Have you had a fight?"

I looked around to make sure nobody was listening, then I told her half the truth. "I think I'm going to dump him ..."

"But why that, all of a sudden?" Franzi didn't understand the world any more.

"I ... um ... I think boys should be faithful!"

Franzi's eyes nearly popped out of her head. "Isn't he? Do you think he's being unfaithful? Who with?"

Thank God Greetje and Lea crossed our path at that moment, and I could put Franzi off with a "not now, more later".

It didn't **suit** her, but since her love of secrets was at least as **pronounced** as her desire for sensation, she **contained** her curiosity.

Unlike me, she had evidently recovered from her shock at Raffi's farewell text pretty well. At any rate, she was **pursuing** precisely the opposite of my **avoidance** strategy. She went up to Raffi on the offensive, gave him a friendly smile, made some joke or another about the class trip and generally acted as if she hadn't received the terrible news.

Not a bad tactic, actually. Why couldn't I do it like

---

to beat around the bush – um den heißen Brei herumreden;
to suit – passen; pronounced – ausgeprägt; to contain – zügeln;
to pursue – verfolgen; avoidance – Vermeidung

that? Did I really have to have seen what had happened? Yes! I had to! Anyone who wanted me to be his girlfriend had to admit the truth to me and act decently. That person's arm had no reason to be on another girl's sleeping bag. And that was that! I was conservative **on that score**.

However, things did turn bad when we were working on the revue with Uschi, and Meik constantly **sought me out**. **Off the cuff**, we put together kissing scenes involving the world's great lovers in literature, films, music and theatre, which of course turned into great fun. It started with Adam and Eve, which immediately sparked off a discussion about whether Adam had kissed Eve before or after she bit into the apple.

"After, of course," said Franzi. "I've got a book which says that kissing is presumed to have arisen because of **pre-mastication**."

"Pre-mastication? That sounds disgusting!"

"Primeval people and primitive people of the modern age," Franzi continued, "did it as a form of **weaning**. They didn't have electric **hand-blenders** to puree stuff, so they just chewed up solid food and pushed it into their babies' mouths." Well, that didn't sound very tasty.

"Yuck!" said Raffi. Kissing as a form of feeding babies didn't seem to turn him on very much.

---

on that score – was das betrifft;
to seek sb out – jmds. Nähe suchen;
off the cuff – aus dem Stegreif; pre-mastication – Vorkauen;
weaning – Abstillen; hand-blender – Handmixer

"Well, as to whether Eve chewed the apple up for Adam, I don't know. He was already well out of babyhood by then ..." Fabian voiced his doubts.

"But it'd make a funny scene if Eva fed Adam mouth-to-mouth with bits of apple," said van Gogh.

"Of course it would," Mona agreed. "First of all Adam and Eve with the apple, then **Lady and the Tramp** with the spaghetti ...!"

"Some kinds of apes still feed their **infants** from mouth to mouth," Franzi shared her lexical knowledge around still further. Whereupon Uschi laughed and, looking across at Fabian, suggested, "Maybe we could get the Gorillas to do an ape scene, and lead from that into the great lovers of world literature."

It was obvious! The next thing we did was **gather together** on the blackboard lovers from film history, although we didn't get very far. Of course we immediately thought of *Titanic, Gone with the Wind, Romeo and Juliet, Sleeping Beauty* and *Snow White,* but Uschi said we should go and have a systematic search on the Internet.

When we then started to act out some of the scenes from memory, nobody could stop laughing. The atmosphere was so brilliant that I had almost given in and forgiven Meik when Mona suddenly ran up to him and demanded that he absolutely had to try out a scene with her. *Gone with the Wind,* of all things: Scarlett O'Hara and Rhett Butler! A kiss that made film history.

Lady and the Tramp – Susi und Strolch; infant – Kind;
to gather together – sammeln

"Clark Gable's breath smelt **vile**," I said **insolently**, but loudly enough for everyone to hear.

Whereupon Mona answered pertly, "Meik's doesn't!"

Grr.

At least I was then allowed to act out Leonardo di Caprio and Kate Winslet on the Titanic with Bastian whilst the jazz combo provided the background music. As his lips brushed mine gently, a soft shiver ran through me. Wow, what a **sublime** moment! It **strengthened** my **resolve** to go to Bastian's party at all costs and try my luck with him.

I stole a glance at Meik. An intense, questioning look from his blue eyes met me. Pah! He could **jolly well** work out why I was angry. Maybe he'd work it out for himself at some point. If he then came crawling back full of **remorse**, I could still decide whether I might want to forgive him. But maybe I wouldn't want to! That all depended on how things went between Bastian and me.

"This is going to be brilliant fun!" said Lea as we left the music room. "The people at the summer party will all be on our side, and Biedermann will have no choice but to withdraw her kissing ban."

Sweeping the playground with Meik that day took place **amidst** an icy silence. Now he was evidently offended as well. And he didn't have the slightest reason to be either.

---

vile – eklig; insolent – frech; sublime – erhaben;
to strengthen – verstärken; resolve – Entschluss;
jolly well – todsicher; remorse – Reue; amidst – unter

When I reached our classroom almost ten minutes late after our "**detention**", I bumped into Wolfie, much to my astonishment. Why was he only just getting here? Had he been wandering helplessly round the building again, having forgotten as he so often did in which classroom he was supposed to be teaching?

He looked past me, embarrassed, and stammered, "Erm, urgent discussion with the headmistress …"

Aha. Well, at least he couldn't **have a go at** me for being late.

We used our computer studies lesson to **trawl** the Internet for film kisses. We found a list of the 100 best love films and printed it out. We were going to meet at Franzi's later, where we could decide which scenes from which films we wanted to include in our revue.

"It'd be best to **rent** a couple of nights in a **video studio**," Lea suggested.

"I reckon if we've got six to eight scenes, that ought to be enough," I said. "We can share them out and make notes on them."

"Oh no," protested Lea, "I want to see them all! I love romantic films!"

A romantic soul. Hopefully real life wouldn't disappoint her too hideously later on! Unlike me. **Snivel**!

---

detention – Nachsitzen; to have a go at sb – jmdn. anpflaumen;
to trawl – *hier:* stöbern; to rent – mieten;
video studio – Videothek; snivel – schnief

After school all the Pepper Dollies went to Franzi's, and we quickly agreed on the most interesting film scenes.

Along with *Gone With The Wind, Titanic, Romeo And Juliet, Shakespeare In Love, Casablanca, Superman, Pretty Woman, You've Got Mail, Star Wars* and *Goldfinger,* Greetje also insisted on *Otto – The Love Movie* and I demanded that we absolutely had to include *Nanny* off the TV as well. Franzi said we should include *Spiderman* – climbing, kissing, **stickiness** – for the boys, and a vampire film especially for Fabian. "He loves horror!"

We wanted to **sprinkle** the scenes loosely between sketches on the origins and history of kissing, and to arrange them in a varied way with songs from the charts and musicals such as *West Side Story* and *Beauty and the Beast.*

At the end Mona was to appear as "Her **Maliciousness** Frau Biedermann" and ban kissing.

"But we'll show her that she can't turn back the tide of history," said Franzi. "We'll have Don Carlos appear, and instead of demanding *Sire, give us freedom of thought,* he'll demand *Madame, give us freedom to kiss!"*

We giggled. Franzi kept having the best ideas. Oh well, she was always going to the theatre. Maybe she should become a theatre **director**.

We slurped green tea, **nibbled** rice cakes and rummaged around in the fat tomes from the town archive.

---

stickiness – Klebrigkeit; to sprinkle – einstreuen;
maliciousness – Bösartigkeit; director – Regisseur/in;
to nibble – knabbern

"My goodness, the Americans were terribly **prudish**," Lea said. "It says here that kisses in films weren't allowed to last any longer than three seconds between 1934 and 1960."

"One of Raffi's kisses doesn't last any longer than that now," Franzi said drily.

Well, that was a shock. Particularly because already I wondered what she actually liked about him in those situations. Oh well, maybe his kisses were too short but passionate! What did it say on that advert: ... *it's small. Seems big. And just re-load it for the next kick.*

I found it very depressing that only three of the ten best films on our hit-list had happy endings and that there was always a lot of **rowing**. 260 kissing scenes to 187 arguments. Which told you yet again that it was always the same: kissing and quarrelling. That really was nothing new to me!

"**French kissing** was only ever simulated!" Lea read on. "It was considered to be perverted."

"What's perverted?" asked Greetje.

We looked at one another questioningly. Well, if she wanted to know so precisely ... then we couldn't really give her an answer. Dictionary here we come. Flick, flick ... perfect, periods, Persil ... aha, there it was ... *perverted*!

I read aloud: "*Normally means sexually **deviant**, unnatural, **depraved**!*"

---

prudish – prüde; to row – *hier:* streiten;
French kissing – Zungenkuss; deviant – abweichend;
depraved – verdorben

"I bet Frau Biedermann thinks kissing's perverted, too, and that's why she's banned it!" said Lea.

Yeah, that was obvious, but she wasn't exactly up to date with this attitude. In the media, at any rate, people were constantly kissing – and it was all varieties of kissing.

All I say is: *Kiss my **arse***!

"Did you know that humans give around a hundred thousand kisses during a lifetime?"

"You'd have to start early and live to a ripe old age," Franzi calculated. "So what exactly is a kiss? Is there a definition anywhere? A precise description and definition?"

"Here: *A kiss is a loving collision of the lips during which two people press them intimately and firmly together. A hearty smacking noise is produced when they move apart*. It comes from a 1735 lexicon for virtuous young ladies."

Giggling and lip-smacking.

"We'll have it, it sounds pretty funny," I said. "But is there anything more modern? What does Brockhaus say?"

Franzi went across to her father's study and returned with a Brockhaus volume.

*"Touching a person or thing with the lips as a **mark** of respect, friendship or love,"* she read aloud.

Then I discovered a thrilling new **source** which listed every possible type of kiss: polite kisses, **furtive**

---

arse – Arsch; mark – Zeichen; source – Quelle;
furtive – verstohlen

kisses, suggestive kisses, angry kisses, bloody kisses, passionate kisses, the kiss of death, nose-kisses, moonlight kisses, Judas kisses, brotherly kisses, stolen kisses … the list was as long as your arm and very inspiring!

"Kisses were *the **kindling** of evil desires,* the devil let the witches kiss his backside on Walpurgisnacht, and women could lose their honour if they let anyone steal a kiss from them before they were married!" Franzi summarised.

Oh wow, then the world was **swarming with dishonourable** women!

"These women were, however, allowed to start proceedings against a man who stole a kiss; he could end up with a **fine** or in prison and …" Franzi giggled, "she had the right to **box his ears**. Emperor Carl V is supposed to have got a slap in the face from a kitchen-maid!"

Greetje grinned. "I suggest Fabian and Gracia for that scene! They don't need much practice!" General amused agreement.

"Fantastic!" Franzi was excited. "There's some great stuff for our revue! Uschi will – to stay with our topic – kiss our feet!"

Our Franzi! She was already back on extra-funny form today.

I really did wonder how she managed it despite her row with Raffi.

---

kindling – Zunder; to swarm with – wimmeln von;
dishonourable – ehrlos; fine – Geldstrafe;
to box sb's ears – jmdn. ohrfeigen

I looked at the time. "I've got to go, guys. We've got homework to do!"

As soon as I got home, I'd send Bastian a **reply** to his invitation card. After all, I'd just got enough witty suggestions.

At home, all hell had broken loose. Mum had arranged a **spur-of-the-moment** party and was awaiting some 20 guests in an hour.

She scurried around the kitchen, getting the **crockery** ready and, moreover, nervously awaiting the party service which was supposed to be delivering a selection of cold meats and cheeses.

"What's going on?" asked Joker, and I growled, "Why at home? Couldn't you have a party at work?"

"No, no, not this time!" cried Mum and ran to the bathroom in her bathrobe to give her hair some more brilliance and **vigour** and to transform her daytime make-up into evening make-up by means of thick mascara, dark eyeshadow, bright lipstick and shiny lip-gloss.

"Why all the **palaver**?" I asked. She never made such a fuss about normal after-work parties which took place every now and then.

"Just put a couple of candles on the table!"

The doorbell rang. The guy from the party service came in balancing two silver platters.

---

reply – Antwort; spur of the moment – spontan;
crockery – Geschirr; vigour – Spannkraft;
palaver – Theater

"There are two more to come," he said, and I held on to Snuffles **lest** she went straight for his trouser leg.

"Fetch a few flowers from the garden and arrange them between the plates."

I fetched them. However, I was gradually becoming interested to know why she was making all this fuss. "Have you **hooked** a great **commission**?"

Mum shook her head, but said, "*Commission* no, but *hooked* yes."

She was talking in **riddles**. What else could you hook?

"A fat fish!" suggested Joker.

"Almost got it!" cried Mum, laughing, and hurried upstairs to throw on a chic dress.

My brother and I looked at one another. We both shook our heads.

"She's gone nuts," remarked Joker, though he sounded pretty calm about it.

Oh well, we were used to quite a lot from our mother. She and the guys in the advertising agency lived in another world.

When she came downstairs, she looked fantastic. Every trace of panic had vanished from her, and she beamed at us in **anticipation**. Yet again, she'd got there just in time.

"The first guests will be here in ten minutes," she said, "that's just enough time for a little espresso."

---

lest – dass nicht; to hook – *hier:* an Land ziehen;
commission – Auftrag; riddle – Rätsel; anticipation – Vorfreude

"I'll make it if you tell me who you've hooked."

"Just think," she **teased** me. "It was 15 years ago … the first **swallows** had just arrived and were building their nests …"

Oh no! She didn't mean …

"Wedding anniversary!" twigged Joker, mega-quick yet again. "It's your wedding anniversary today!"

Mum laughed. "Precisely! I'd almost forgotten. If Dad hadn't said he'd be coming home after the session in Berlin, it would have entirely slipped my mind. Even though it's our fifteenth!"

"And so you've quickly organised a surprise party?!" I asked, full of astonishment.

When Dad arrived at the front door later that evening, a happy crowd of guests greeted him. "Surprise!!!"

It was **priceless**. Of course the party went on until the early hours. I, however, didn't stay up for it.

At some point at around midnight my brother was sent to bed, and I followed him **of my own accord** a bit later. After all, I had to go to school the next day.

From my room, I could still hear Mum and Dad laughing with their guests.

Fascinating. Even after 15 years, including quite a lot of stress and rows at work and at home, they still seemed to love one another. And yet they were such different types. Maybe it was precisely that, though, that made them still seem interesting to one another.

---

to tease sb – jmdn. necken; swallow – Schwalbe;
priceless – *hier:* unvergleichlich; of my own accord – freiwillig

This thought reminded me of my problem with Meik which the day's **diversions** had suppressed to some extent. Lying now alone in my bed, hearing the faint music and the laughter of the party guests drifting over, the pain arose slowly and bitterly within me again. And when I then reached for my mobile which had lain ignored on my bedside table all evening, I discovered that he'd texted me at ten p.m. And then I almost started to cry, because he'd written:

I'm sending a text to your mobile
because I don't want you to forget me.
But I'd rather be in your heart
because mobiles can get lost.
Sweetheart, what's wrong with you?

What's wrong with you? Huh! He hadn't understood a thing! And if he loved me that much, why didn't he **hesitate** to play Rhett Butler for Mona? He'd have sunk on the Titanic with me if he really loved me.

I couldn't sleep. So I got up and sat at the computer again. I had quite forgotten to send Bastian a reply to his birthday invitation. When I logged in, I immediately saw that there was an e-mail for M-lieschen. He really didn't waste any time.

I opened the file and almost fell off my chair. Scarlett O'Hara and Rhett Butler were staring at me from an old film poster. **Clutching** one another tightly in a three-second film kiss in close-up and technicolour. Where on earth had he found that?

---

diversion – Ablenkung; to hesitate – zögern; to clutch – umarmen

At first I thought it very sweet until I remembered to my horror that I wasn't the one who'd acted in this scene but Mona – and with my Meik **to boot**! Of course, that made sense of the text that he'd written underneath:

I'd love to be Rhett Butler …

Nothing about Leonardo, nothing about Kate Winslet – nothing about Titanic. He wanted something from Mona, not from me! I had to face this horrible fact. Maybe he'd already fallen for her and I'd just helped him along with my stupid e-mails. Just in order to get rid of Mona. An idea that was in itself truly brilliant. After all, I couldn't have guessed that things would develop so chaotically and that I would end up not only getting rid of Mona but Meik, too!

All of a sudden, Mum was standing in my room. "I saw your light was still on," she said by way of explanation. "What are you doing, still on the computer? Can't it wait until tomorrow? You should have been asleep ages ago." And she added self-critically, "Or are we too loud for you?"

I shook my head and said in a **wobbly** voice, "No, no, it's fine."

She came closer, held my chin and turned my face towards her. "You're crying," she said, genuinely concerned. "What's the matter? Are you ill?"

I shook my head silently again. She pulled me from my chair over to my bed. Once we were sitting close together there, my frustration dissolved and became a real howling session.

---

to boot – noch dazu; wobbly – zittrig

Mum took me in her arms to comfort me, and stroked my hair. "What is it, child? Tell me what's on your mind."

After a while, I'd cried myself out and I just felt sorry that I'd spoilt Mum's fun evening for her.

"You've not spoilt anything," she said when I apologised. "But I can't help you if you don't tell me what it's all about." Well, she was probably right there.

"It's about fidelity," I finally said.

"Oh," she said. "Well that really is a serious topic."

I raised my head and looked at her with **moist** eyes. "Have you and Dad always been faithful to one another?"

She didn't answer immediately. "Before or after we got married?" she finally asked.

I sensed something terrible. "Was he unfaithful?"

"Why him?" she asked with a **mischievous** undertone.

She's drunk, I thought, or at least a bit tipsy; she's not taking it seriously. But she was. She was in fact astonishingly clear-headed and summed up the whole business in her **customary** way.

"Fidelity is relative," she said. "So long people choose it and it doesn't **hem them in**, it's fine and an important basis for a relationship. But what's more important in my opinion is trust."

"But they go together!"

---

moist – feucht; mischievous – verschmitzt;
customary – typisch; to hem sb in – jmdn. einengen

"Depends how you see it. There are some situations in life where you might get to know someone whom you're desperate to get together with. Someone you find attractive, likeable, yes, maybe even sexually attractive, but with whom you'd never have a permanent relationship, never mind marry them or have children with them. Your father and I have always known that we'd only do that with one another, nobody else. And we've always trusted that nothing and nobody could change that."

"Nothing and nobody?"

"Nothing and nobody! We'd hardly still be together after 15 years otherwise."

I barely dared to say it, but I had to know. "So you weren't always faithful to one another?"

Mum looked me straight in the eye. "No, not always. We were often apart because of work, and we both had to fight our way and go through tough times until we got to where we wanted to be. So we were glad to have other people to support us and pick up all our stress and give us security."

"And you weren't jealous?"

"Yes and no. Let's say, it's a bit painful when you find out about it. Somehow you do tend to view your partner as your own property. But that's the **gut feeling**; you can get your head round it so long as the basic rules of the game aren't broken. And anyway, we always had a common goal and the trust that we'd get there at some

---

gut feeling – Bauchgefühl

point. And then we soon had you and your brother. From then onwards, our family was always the prime thing."

As she spoke, Mum had stared ahead of her rather absently. Now she looked at me again. "Am I right in supposing that you've got a fidelity problem with Meik?"

I nodded. She was too clever for anyone to hide anything from her for long.

"And you're jealous, very jealous – is that right?"

"Yes, that's right. But I think it's just because of Mona! No boy can resist her, and now Meik's after her as well …"

"Are you quite sure? He's surely not the type. Maybe you've misunderstood something about his behaviour?"

Misunderstood? What was there to misunderstand about your boyfriend's hand being on another girl's sleeping bag?

Dad stuck his head round the door. "Oh, you're here. The guests are wondering where you've got to!"

Mum stood up. "I'll be there in a minute!" And to me she said, "Talk to him before you do anything **rash** that you'll regret later. I think he's a really nice and decent boy." And she added with a wink, "A true **mother-in-law's** dream!"

At the door she turned once more and said seriously, "If I can help … mediate between you or whatever, do let me know."

---

rash – voreilig; mother-in-law – Schwiegermutter

Stolen Kisses

Next morning, I felt completely whacked.

I didn't understand the world any more. My boyfriend had **betrayed** me and my mother had told me that this was evidently quite normal and happened even in a good marriage like my parents'. I couldn't believe it.

Surely love meant being completely and **utterly** devoted to one's beloved for ever and eternity. You couldn't just go messing around with other people! I thought, at any rate, that I could only really love one person and if he didn't love me just as **inalienably** and exclusively, then he wasn't the right boy for me. Or was I living on a different planet?

... and then I go and spoil it all by saying something stupid like I love you ...

For God's sake, I believed in great love! Was that forbidden?

---

to betray – betrügen; utter – total; inalienable – unveräußerlich

On my way to school, my problem had turned somewhat into this question. If I believed in great love, that didn't necessarily mean that I would find it only with Meik. If he was scurrying around after Mona, then at the end of the day, there were other boys, too. And one of them was Bastian. If I'd turned him on via e-mail as M-lieschen, then I could turn him off again as M-lieschen, too. As Mona, I could turn down his invitation and turn up at the party myself. Then we'd see whether I – with chic styling and my professional model's way of walking – couldn't blow my rival out of the water. And if I then admitted that I was the one he'd been exchanging sweet e-mails with … that kind of spiritual **affinity** had to count for more than a backside, however great it was!

With new self-confidence, I faced whatever the day had in store for me.

However, it wasn't terribly positive.

Our Maths teacher Logel set us a test that brought me to the **brink** of despair, and Frau Ingrimm demanded the **minutes** of the lesson that I'd somehow completely forgotten about. **To add insult to injury**, Birkenstock asked for the name of the twelve **disciples** of whom I could name only five, and there was spinach with mashed potatoes and fried eggs for lunch. Ugh!

How did a morning like that **bode** for the rest of the day? Badly! Precisely!

---

affinity – Verwandtschaft; brink – Rand; minute – Protokoll; to add insult to injury – zu allem Übel; disciples – Jünger; to bode – verheißen

And so I was walking to the art room with Franzi in a somewhat foul mood when Meik was suddenly standing in front of me in the corridor, blocking my way.

"Let me through!" I said stroppily.

"Only if you pay me a **ransom**!"

"Like what?"

"Well, the local **currency** – a kiss!"

"Kissing's forbidden on the school premises."

He grinned ironically.

"However could I forget?" Completely unimpressed by Frau Biedermann's regulations, he made his mouth into a kiss shape.

"We've already had two warnings! Let me get past – I don't want a black mark on my report."

Franzi looked at me with irritation at my **ferocity**.

"There's no one looking," she whispered to me. "You can trust me."

Well, she was being a great help yet again. Had I asked her for support? No! If I wanted to kiss Meik, I'd have done it with or without a ban. And I couldn't have given a toss whether Franzi or Frau Biedermann had seen or not.

But I didn't want to!

But he wanted to. And before I knew what was happening, he'd taken me in his arms and had stolen a kiss from me.

"Well, does my breath smell, Scarlett O'Hara?" he said after almost exactly three seconds. And he just left

---

ransom – Lösegeld; currency – Währung; ferocity – Heftigkeit

me standing there with a perfect film kiss and the aftertaste of fresh mint on my lips.

I liked Meik's kisses, but him – I didn't like him at all any more, and so after school I immediately got stuck into transforming my mega-brilliant strategy into action: getting Mona **out of the running** with Bastian.

I wanted to go to his party and throw myself at him **come hell or high water**.

But, but, my inner governess was making herself heard. *Nice girls don't do that kind of thing.*

"Maybe not," I retorted pertly. "But as we all know, nice girls don't get anywhere, and bad girls do. I'm sick of being nice and all alone. I'd rather be a bit less nice and have lots of admirers instead."

And as I logged into my mailbox, I trilled softly, *"Boys gather around me like* ***moths*** *to a light..."*

Well, it looks like we've done it. M-lieschen! I'd get rid of her now. Should I use the **sledgehammer** method and say something along the lines of: I made a mistake, you're not the right guy; or should I tell him **in a roundabout way**?

Hmm, Mona herself would presumably do it clearly but kindly. She never hurt anyone by being directly unfriendly. Unlike me, she had complete control of herself and could withdraw from situations. But when she did

---

out of the running – aus dem Rennen;
come hell or high water – auf Teufel komm raus;
moth – Motte; sledgehammer – Holzhammer;
in a roundabout way – durch die Blume

so, she was nevertheless often completely uncompromising.

Right, I thought, imagine I'm Mona and I've started to find Bastian tiresome because I've fallen in love with Meik.

Sniff! What reply should I give to Bastian's birthday invitation? *Can I bring Meik with me?* No, that was too mean. Some excuse. *It's my great-grandparents' golden wedding anniversary.*

Well, not exactly brilliant. My **gaze** fell on the newspaper. It was Thursday, and it was open at the horoscope page.

I had an idea. What if I produced a mega-bad horoscope for Bastian's birthday, warning him of a good-looking red-headed woman? Mona could have read it and decided to **cry off** going to the party in view of it. Just because she didn't want to bring him misfortune. He'd understand and be grateful, but would steer clear of her, for who liked to put himself in danger? Brilliant. That's what I'd do.

I found a lovely greetings card with Bastian's star sign on it, and then I **crafted** a hideous horoscope under it. The **gist**: steer clear of red-headed women for the next year, or you'll regret it.

I chose a purple font and then read it all through once more. Hmm, there could easily be something a bit more constructive at the end. Perhaps a gentle **hint** that a sur-

---

gaze – Blick;
to cry off – *hier:* absagen;
to craft – erstellen; gist – Hauptaussage; hint – Hinweis

prise guest would bring great happiness. I was, of course, thinking of myself.

Was that too direct? **Too much of a giveaway**? No. So long as I didn't immediately start mentioning a blonde woman ... Surprise guest sounded neutral and he would notice in good time that I was that guest ...

So I added another sentence to my text and then sent the message. Adieu, Monalieschen, Bastian won't be interested in you any more – but he'll soon be interested in me. I'd make damn sure of that at the party the next evening. I just had to hope that he believed in horoscopes a bit.

He evidently didn't. For when I got to his house seriously **dolled up**, wearing a **crop top** and with my hair up, my **jaw** almost dropped to the floor. Who else but Mona was laughing by his side and digging in to the cold buffet.

I just didn't get it! What was she doing here? How did she know about the invitation? He'd sent it to me, to my disguise e-mail address. There was nothing for it: I had to find out what was going on.

As elegantly as possible, I walked over to the buffet and as a friend was just talking to Bastian, I placed myself inconspicuously next to Mona.

"Hi, Mona," I said in a deliberately relaxed way. "Nice party. Didn't know you were invited as well."

Too much of a giveaway? – Zu verräterisch?;
to doll up – sich aufbrezeln; crop top – bauchnabelfreies Top;
jaw – Kiefer; *hier:* Kinnlade

At that moment I could have bitten my tongue out. What kind of stupid introduction was that?

But she just grinned and said, "Yes, I didn't know about it either until this morning, but Bastian approached me at break and asked if I believed in horoscopes. I hadn't got **the faintest idea** what he was getting at. But since I think horoscopes are stupid anyway, I, of course, said no. And then he said that everything was fine and that I could come to his birthday party this evening. And that he didn't believe in them either."

I, of course, hadn't expected that. Neither that he didn't believe in horoscopes nor that he'd be bold enough to talk directly to Mona about the e-mail.

"I didn't get it, it's true, but you know me: I'm not going to turn down a party invitation."

She had loaded up her plate with **delicacies**. "Great that you're here, too, Kiki," she said, diplomatically shaking me off. "I'm going to have something to eat now; see you later."

And she'd gone. When I saw her next, she was cheerfully chewing and laughing with Bastian and a couple of his mates at a table near the garden pond.

My hands trembled with anger, and I had to put my plate and glass down quickly on one of the side tables. I looked around in frustration. There was nobody there that I knew. Of course I'd seen a lot of the people in the school playground, but they were all in Year Nine, and didn't normally socialise with Year Sevens. Why they

---

the faintest idea – die leiseste Ahnung; delicacy – Köstlichkeit

made an exception with Mona was, yet again, a complete mystery to me.

I left my food where it was, as I wouldn't have been able to force down a single mouthful anyway, and went into the house to find a toilet.

Bastian's family evidently wasn't one of the poorer ones.

An elegantly dressed lady approached me in the doorway.

"Can I help you?" she said in a pleasant voice.

"Erm, yes, I'm looking for the toilet."

She directed me towards the guest loo and shortly afterwards I was standing in a **twinkling** and sparkling **marble** washroom with wall-height mirrors above the wash basin and effective indirect lighting.

Was it clever light management or the softly **tinted** mirror glass? When I looked in the mirror, I thought I was actually pretty good-looking.

"Fantastic," I said to myself. "You look fantastic, Kiki. Like at the fashion show and at least 16. If the boy doesn't bite, he doesn't deserve you!"

With a new self-confidence, I threw myself into the battle for Bastian.

But before I'd found him, my self-confidence had pretty much evaporated. For the girls from his year who he'd invited were all good-looking. And there was one thing that couldn't be ignored: most of them had decidedly more in their blouses than I had. All the same, a

---

twinkling – funkelnd; marble – Marmor; tinted – getönt

couple of boys spoke to me, but I didn't let myself get involved in any long conversations because I wanted to find Bastian. And finally I was lucky. He was squatting on the other side of the garden pond and seemed to be fiddling with some part of the mechanism. I went over to him and took it as the starting point for a conversation.

"What are you doing?"

"Oh, I'm just switching on the lighting and the fountain," he said. "Good to see you. How did you know about the party? Did Mona bring you with her?"

It didn't get much more embarrassing than that. How was I supposed to flirt with him now, when he'd said straight to my face that he hadn't invited me? That meant quite clearly that he'd never had the slightest private interest in me despite the kissing scenes he was acting out with me in the revue. How shameful! My throat felt as if it were **tied in knots**. I couldn't get a single word out. Spaghetti can't speak either, I thought, and people love it all the same. Maybe he actually liked silent girls. A moment later, thank God, the pond fountain hissed upwards, and a colourful light body under the surface of the water bathed it in constantly changing colours.

"Wonderful!" Mona's voice suddenly rang out behind us, and then she was already standing next to him. She linked arms with him and chatted merrily as she watched the waterworks. **Waffle**, waffle!

---

to be tied in knots – zugeschnürt sein;
Waffle! – Schwafel!

I slipped away **unobtrusively**. In a **dimly lit** corner I bumped into a boy who'd already approached me earlier. He was called Bernhard and he invited me for a beer. Mum had in fact forbidden alcohol, but if Bastian's parents allowed it ...

As it turned out, however, this Bernhard was **self-sufficient**. He proudly showed me two six-packs that he'd just bought from the kiosk. If the truth is in wine, then maybe it's in beer, too, I thought. Well, I prescribed myself a **mind-expanding** swig. As my personal route to enlightenment, so to speak. The eighth Tibetan or such like. Maybe my mood might improve after all the frustration.

Bernhard passed me a bottle. "Alcohol, you **evil spirit**," he declared as he did so, "even if you knock me down today, I'll get up; knock me down again and I'll puke you out and drink you again. Cheers!"

I giggled and then clung to him for the time being. He forced another bottle upon me. But after I'd initially kept up with him for a while, I stopped enjoying the taste completely and I began discreetly to **dispose of** the contents of the bottle into the undergrowth.

The six-packs were gradually emptied and Bernhard became more and more drunk. He told me his whole life-story and I told him everything about the history of kissing. The fact that this didn't remotely give him

---

unobtrusive – unauffällig; dim lit – schummrig;
self-sufficient – *hier:* Selbstversorger;
mind-expanding – bewusstseinserweiternd;
evil spirit – böser Geist; to dispose of sth – etwas loswerden

the idea of making any kind of advance in this direction either said nothing for him or nothing for me. I finally felt that I was casting pearls before **swine** and, **bored stiff**, returned to the buffet.

I shovelled a large portion of vanilla pudding onto a plate and splashed a generous **ladle** of red sauce on top.

A girl tapped me on the arm. "Hey, that's not red fruit pudding. It's ketchup."

Whoops, how embarrassing! Just don't let anyone notice. "Of course I know. Vanilla pudding with ketchup is the latest thing. However, it could do with a **pinch** of curry powder and a **dash** of Tabasco …"

The girl stared at me as if I were a **corn-circle** alien. "Are you **pregnant** or what?"

I retreated into a dark corner and **fertilised** Bastian's garden once more. Wow, would there ever be a **growth spurt** there soon!

Then I decided to tackle the business with Bastian again. I'd simply explain to him that Mona was messing around with Meik as well. Then he'd be bound to have had enough of her, and he'd be very keen to get involved with me.

As I approached Bastian, I had a feeling that I was a bit **unsteady** on my legs and that I couldn't walk in an entirely straight line. How much beer had I actually drunk? Oh, whatever. So long as I could still think clear-

---

swine – Schwein; bored stiff – *hier:* angeödet; ladle – Schöpflöffel;
pinch – Prise; dash – Spritzer; corn-circle – Kornkreis;
pregnant – schwanger; to fertilise – düngen;
growth spurt – Wachstumsexplosion; unsteady – unsicher

ly, that made no difference. But I presumably wasn't really that clear-headed after all, and we all know that language is given to humans so they can hide their thoughts. At least I could manage that one brilliantly!

"Lovely goldfish you've got in your pond! Really very goldy."

Bastian gave me a rather irritated look and corrected me. "They're Japanese grass carp."

Know-all!

"Oh," I **ventured** a joke. "Have you put grass in the pond? Load of **pot-heads**, eh?"

He didn't respond.

"Have you had one glass too many, little one?" he asked instead, though I only heard something about "eating grass" and asked for my part, "Oh, can you eat it as well? I thought you smoked it!"

I somehow felt as if I'd already **inhaled** a joint myself, and thought, *gentle clouds are lifting me up*. And so I started singing with complete abandon Stefan Raab's pot-song that my brother kept bellowing under the shower and that I in fact found absolutely dreadful: *"And Boris Becker, that's **encouraging**, was only really good on grass … We're smoking pot …"*

I don't know if I'd suddenly touched upon a delicate topic in the light of the sudden appearance of his mother – "Our son hasn't got a drug-problem" or such like – but at any rate, Bastian seemed to find the direction our

---

know-all – Besserwisser; to venture – wagen; pot-head – Kiffer; to inhale – inhalieren; encouraging – ermutigend

conversation had taken very unpleasant. He grabbed me rather firmly by the arm and said, "You'd better have a coffee, and I'll call you a taxi in the meantime."

But on principle I didn't let anyone grab me by the arm. So it was a reflex, really, that made me pull away from him and simultaneously push him off. A simple trick from the *Self-Defence For Girls* club. Often tried out, but never yet put into practice! Unexpectedly effective as well. A loud splash instantly silenced the general party **murmur**.

Oh my goodness, what had I done? If I was seeing rightly, I'd chucked Bastian – our host, the birthday boy, the one I fancied, our student head – into his garden pond with a well-aimed ju-jitsu trick. Wow! He was now paddling around, **snorting**, between the water-lilies and grass carp, and made an extremely funny sight. He, however, didn't seem the slightest bit amused. As he pulled himself up on the edge of the pond, he **clenched his teeth**. It wasn't entirely clear whether it was with rage or cold, but it didn't really matter either.

He's going to kill me, I thought, but was incapable of moving.

He ran past me, dripping, and fixed me with a murderous look. As he did so, I could hear him hissing, "Horoscopes! Pah! Why didn't anyone warn me about a blonde lunatic instead of a red-head!"

In order to save my parents the **funeral** costs, I de-

---

murmur – Gemurmel; to snort – prusten;
to clench one's teeth – die Zähne zusammenbeißen;
funeral – Beerdigung

cided to leave the party as quickly as possible. Without having a coffee, I slipped through a back gate and stumbled down the road in a more or less straight line. After all, it wasn't that far to the bus.

I could even see the bus stop already. Once at the **shelter**, I dropped down onto the bench. After I'd rested for a while, I stood up and tried to read the timetable. It appeared that I might have to wait a while for the next bus to come.

So I decided to walk a bit further.

Mum had, it's true, said that I should never walk around on my own in the evenings as it was too dangerous, but what could happen to me? And I could hardly ask someone at the party to take me home like a little child.

You could have done the normal thing and phoned for a taxi, my inner governess said **disapprovingly**.

"Maybe I'll be lucky and a taxi might just happen to drive past," I said to my over-anxious virtual guardian. But no taxi came; not even so much as another car drove down this pretty isolated road.

So I walked and walked and soon had the feeling that I'd come to an area that I'd never been to before in my life. It looked a bit too **neat** and tidy for my taste. Presumably, the people who lived here were totally **pernickety** and **vacuumed** their front gardens and **dusted** their letter-boxes every Saturday. Now they all seemed

---

shelter – *hier:* Wartehäuschen; disapproving – missbilligend;
neat – gepflegt; pernickety – kleinlich, pingelig;
to vacuum – staubsaugen; to dust – abstauben

to be asleep or to be sitting around in front of the box. Oh well, at least they hadn't folded up the pavements yet.

A group of pedestrians, presumably not from this area either, came towards me talking loudly and laughing. Slightly anxious, I squeezed past them.

I suddenly heard the dynamo of a bicycle humming behind me, and its lights threw my shadow blackly at my feet. I turned round.

"Hey, Kiki," said the cyclist to me, stopping abruptly.

"Fabian? What are you doing here?" I said, relieved. He appeared as a rescuing angel!

"I live here. I'm just coming back from football training. And what about you? Where've you been?"

"I ... I ... was at a party. It's Bastian's birthday."

Fabian got off his bike and pushed it along beside me. He sniffed the air. "Well, you're a bit tanked up," he said with a grin.

I didn't immediately get it. "You what?"

"You've had too much to drink," he said more clearly.

Crikey, was that boy ever **loutish**. I remembered exactly why I always steered clear of him and his Gorillas.

All of a sudden, I didn't feel particularly comfortable in his company.

"Are you afraid?" Fabian said, again very directly.

Like hell would I give him a truthful answer. Of course I was afraid. "Naah, why should I be?"

---

loutish – flegelhaft; like hell – nicht im mindesten

"Do you want me to take you home?"

"Naah, you really don't need to," I refused gratefully. Then I had the perfect answer. "I can order a taxi from here on my mobile." Why hadn't I immediately thought of that? Really must be the alcohol to **blame**, those little devils in the bottle who cause chaos in the human mind once they're let loose.

I pulled out my mobile. At some point, I'd programmed in the number of a taxi firm. I was just about to call the number when Fabian put his hand on mine. He'd leaned his bike against one of the alley trees. **Angel my foot**!

"You can do that later," he said in an unnaturally soft voice. "You look fantastic tonight, Kiki. You know I've fancied you for ages."

Then he pulled me towards him with his strong arms and tried to kiss me.

For a moment I was seized by real panic. What on earth could I do in this dark, godforsaken area to get rid of him? If I did the wrong thing and he turned angry at being **rebuffed**, there was nobody to help me. His hot breath stroked my face, then his lips touched my cheek. I turned my face away. My God, he'd presumably remembered about our kissing revue! Where else could he have got the idea of attacking me? I'd never given him any reason to think that I had even the faintest **trace** of interest in him! But we all knew it: when opportunity knocks ...! I became angry. And my anger to-

---

to blame – die Schuld geben; Angel my foot. – Von wegen Engel.; to be rebuffed – eine Abfuhr bekommen; trace – Spur

wards this would-be *kissing-opportunist,* who was trying to take advantage of my situation, turned rather violent.

I wasn't so drunk that I couldn't see what was going on around me. He really was out of his head if he thought he could **lay** me just like that, just because I'd drunk a bit of beer. I straightened up internally and then externally. Should I immediately try ju-jitsu again which I – as I'd shown in the case of Bastian – had evidently mastered perfectly, or start off with a verbal strike?

"Get your paws off me!" I shouted at him, instinctively adding, "or Meik will make **mincemeat** of you at school tomorrow!"

That worked. He let go of me.

"Okay, okay," he said, sounding **huffy**. "There are plenty of girls who fancy me. But if you don't want it ..."

"Meik's really jealous. If he gets wind of something, he'll **do you in**!"

That did it. Fabian took his bike.

"You don't have to tell him absolutely everything," he said. "Do you want me to wait for the taxi to come? It's a bit of an unsafe area."

Well, he was a joker. Who'd made the area unsafe?! But I accepted his offer as he seemed to be pretty normal again and evidently wanted to erase the bad impression he'd just made. Terrible, these uncontrollable

---

to lay – *hier:* vernaschen; mincemeat – Hackfleisch;
huffy – eingeschnappt; to do sb in – jmdn. umbringen

surges of desire that boys have! They really should offer a club at school where boys learnt to deal with their urges constructively. I dialled the taxi headquarters. Five minutes later, the taxi arrived.

"Keep it between ourselves?" asked Fabian as we parted. He must be terrified of Meik.

I nodded. "But kindly keep your hands off me in future."

In the taxi, I then felt pretty ill. Wow, that wasn't going to happen to me again. Alone at night in a strange area. If you put yourself in danger ... Well, it had all turned out okay. Trembling slightly I gave the taxi driver his euros, then climbed out and **tottered** towards our house.

There was still a light on downstairs. Of course Mum mostly got home late or stayed up for a long time.

Damn. I didn't particularly want to **encounter** her in my **current** state, so I crept along the wall of the house to my brother's room.

I tapped softly on the window. "Joker, hey, Joker, wake up." Nothing **stirred**. I knocked more loudly. "Hey, you **sloth**, wake up!!!"

I took a **pebble** and tapped it on the aluminium window ledge. A light went on next door. My goodness, didn't they have sharp ears.

"What's going on down there?" cried Frau Waschlapski.

---

surge – Wallung; to totter – wanken; to encounter – treffen; current – momentan; to stir – *hier:* sich rühren; sloth – Faultier; pebble – Kieselstein

"Erm, erm, nothing," I said, waving her aside. "It's not intended for you."

Why had she just had her **hearing aid** switched on then, but not now? Purely in order to **harass** me!

"It's me, Kristina!" I added in order to make clear to her that I wasn't some burglar or something.

"Does your mother allow you out so late?"

I'd say probably not, I thought, and called in a low voice, "The key to our front door's broken, so I've got to get in through the window."

"What's broken? Why are you smashing the window?"

She doesn't get it, I thought despairingly, and if she carries on **nagging**, the whole neighbourhood will soon be awake. I had to disappear at once.

I left Frau Waschlapski to her dark speculations for a moment and knocked on my brother's window once more.

"Wake up, for goodness' sake, you sleepy-head!" I moaned as I did so.

The window finally opened. One half-asleep brother looked at me uncomprehendingly. "Kiki? What are you doing here?"

"In! Let me in! Quickly!"

"Is someone after you?"

"Yes, Frau Waschlapski! Now make space!"

"Why don't you use the door?"

"Can't. I don't want to run into Mum."

---

hearing aid – Hörgerät; to harass – ärgern;
to nag – keifen, nörgeln

Joker sniffed the air. "Wow, you've done a bit too much saving of the rainforest. You're drunk!" he stated. "Well, come on in."

I called to Frau Waschlapski: "Good night! Sleep well," threw myself over the window **sill** and pulled myself into the room.

Moments later I was sitting on the floor of my brother's bedroom. Somewhat **out of it**, but safe **nonetheless**.

I watched Frau Waschlapski shaking her head as she closed her window. Then her light went out, too. **Crikey**, just got away with it.

I **hauled myself up**. I carefully opened the **nursery door** a crack and peeped out into the corridor. Once I could be sure that I wouldn't encounter anyone, I crept out with a quietly whispered "thanks".

It was only a few paces to my bedroom, where I locked the door and flopped down onto my bed exactly as I was.

Saved!

I pulled out my mobile and sent Mum a text.

Hi Mum. Just flopped into bed, totally exhausted. Didn't want to ***disturb*** *you. The party was great.*

Kisses,

Kiki

---

sill – *hier:* Brüstung;
to be out of it – *hier:* durch den Wind sein;
nonetheless – immerhin; Crikey! – Da schau her!;
to haul oneself up – sich hochziehen;
nursery door – Kinderzimmertür; to disturb – stören

So. Now she'd be reassured and I wouldn't have to come under her **beady** eyes again. However, she knocked gently on my door once more. "Kiki? Are you still awake?"

I grunted sleepily. "No-oo."

"Was it good? Everything okay with Meik again?"

With Meik? Oh yes, she didn't know that I hadn't been out with Meik but had been to Bastian's birthday party on my own. I hadn't told her at all – **by an oversight**, of course.

"Yes, yes, everything's fine," I replied in order to **nip** further questions **in the bud**. The only thing I needed now was peace and quiet, or I really would be ill. This much was clear: I wouldn't be drinking alcohol again that quickly.

Regardless of whether I was drowning my lovesickness sorrows or anything else, it would be the Queen of Table Waters or Bonaqua Classic for me.

"Okay, sleep well then. And get home a bit earlier next time or text me. I worry about you."

And you're right to worry, I thought. Oh, men!

I promised to do so from my deeper understanding and shut my eyes.

Although I was dog-tired, I couldn't sleep. I stood up and switched the computer on. I checked my inbox mechanically. Had Bastian written to M-lieschen again? After the drama with the lily pond I was, of course, des-

---

beady – scharf;
by an oversight – aus Versehen;
to nip in the bud – im Keim ersticken;

perate to know whether the pair of them had got together. Yes, indeed. A greetings card from Bastinochild had arrived. I opened it with feverish haste.

Under the photo of a single dark red rose, it said:

It's late when I turn off my light.
Shadows paint the moon's ***rays*** *on the wall.*
I see your face in them,
talking to me of love,
and I hear
your laughter
in the night wind,
the laughter
that makes me happy.
Bastian

Wherever he'd stolen it from, it was fabulously beautiful, romantic, in love ... it ... it was simply unbearable! I logged off and got back into bed. I sighed with frustration. Oh, if only that e-mail had really been directed at me! What wouldn't I give for that. I heard Mum **tiptoeing** upstairs to her bedroom, then I dozed off into a restless sleep.

---

ray – Strahl; to tiptoe – auf Zehenspitzen gehen

Ill with Kissing

"Can you show me the trick with the thermometer?" I asked my brother the next morning.

"But of course." He immediately showed his solidarity by cooperating with me and **letting me in on his dodge**.

I crawled back into my bed, pulled the covers over my head and played dead.

When Mum looked at me in astonishment, I adopted an expression of suffering, handed her the thermometer and said, "I'm dying, I think I'm dying!"

"Hmm."

Mum looked at the thermometer then at me. She put her hand on my **forehead**.

"Strange," she murmured, "where did you take your temperature? Your forehead feels perfectly normal."

Blimey, was that woman **sharp**. Oh well, she presumably had to be with my brother. He is constantly

---

to let sb in on one's dodge – jmdm. seinen Trick verraten;
forehead – Stirn; Blimey! – Verdammt!;
sharp – gewitzt

trying to trick her. But how was I supposed to explain the temperature differential between the thermometer and my skin?

Before I could explain anything, Mum looked at me very critically and said, "You're **cheating**. The thermometer's been **interfered with**. Just admit it!"

I **lowered** my gaze guiltily and nodded. "Yes, you're right, but I really do feel baaaad. I definitely ate something bad yesterday." Or, rather, drank something bad, but I was better off keeping that one to myself if I wanted to get any chance of a break today. "Can't I just stay at home today? We've not got any important lessons. Just Geography, RE, Sport ... I'll collapse in that in any case. Do you want that to happen?"

I looked at Mum, begging for sympathy.

But she had her principles and **remained firm**. "Anyone who can spend the night partying can go to school the next morning. And if you're really no better this afternoon, go to the doctor's. Just so you know."

I gave up. Well, this was going to be fun.

What I was **dreading** most was, of course, the rehearsal for the kissing revue. Bastian and Meik as a twin-pack: oh horrors. However, I decided to follow Franzi's example and take the bull by the horns. Goodbye, head-in-the-sand **policy**. And there wasn't really any sand I could stick my head into.

---

to cheat – schwindeln;
to interfere with – manipulieren;
to lower – senken; to remain firm – hart bleiben;
to dread – fürchten; policy – Politik

After the English lesson I fearlessly gathered my stuff together to slip off to the music room. However, I was in no great hurry given everything that was awaiting me. It almost drove Franzi mad.

"Oh, get a move on!" she nagged. She presumably couldn't wait to **coo** lovingly at Raffi.

They seemed to be one heart and one soul again, that pair. I sighed.

"You've got no idea how many times I've put my foot in it!"

She looked at me, full of curiosity. "Where did that happen?"

"At Bastian's birthday party."

"No, I don't believe it! You were there! And you didn't tell me!" She appeared to be genuinely disappointed.

Meanwhile we had reached the music room, and so I lowered my voice and whispered, "Not now; I'll tell you everything later ..."

"In minute detail! Promise?"

I nodded. "Promise."

At the door I did hesitate. He's going to destroy me, I thought. Bastian will ram me **headfirst** into the stage! Franzi pushed me into the room. Oh well, if I was about to meet my **doom**, then I'd do it with attitude. I threw my shoulders back and straightened my **spine**.

---

to coo – gurren;
headfirst – kopfüber;
doom – Schicksal, Untergang;
spine – Wirbelsäule

Bastian was already standing on the stage, moving a couple of tables and chairs around.

Go on, my inner coach encouraged me. *Get stuck in. Self is the woman!*

I mounted the stage through the back entrance and forced myself to walk straight across to Bastian, upright and using my most stylish model's way of walking.

"You don't really hate me," I said as I stood before him.

He raised his eyebrows in astonishment. God, did that ever look cute. And before he could recover from his astonishment and make any kind of reply, I grabbed his hand and put it on his mouth. Just as Tom Hanks did with Meg Ryan in *You've Got Mail.*

"What's that all about?" Bastian mumbled through his fingers.

"I'm stopping you from saying something that you might regret for the whole of the rest of your life."

He evidently remembered the film scene now, for he grinned as he took his hand away from his mouth. "What makes you think I could hate you?"

"Have you forgotten? I'm the crazy blonde who kicked you into the lily pond at your birthday party. If that's not a reason to hate someone ..."

A diabolical **spark** appeared in Bastian's eyes. Now he's going to go for my throat, I thought in horror, but he just said with a faintly ironic undertone, "Yes, I really could have something to say about that, but you've just forbidden me."

---

spark – Funkeln

I was perplexed. "You're not going to murder me?"

The **roguish** smile once again. This time it flashed across his whole face. "Should I?"

I took a step backwards, but ventured another huge advance with my next sentence. "Can you forgive me? I normally **chat** guys **up** a bit more gently but, I don't know, in your case, something must have **disabled the laws of gravity**. Completely abnormal **repulsion** ..."

He grinned and as he evidently had plenty of **grey matter** where science was concerned, he immediately took up the metaphor. "Well, that means that we're of a similar polarity, speaking in terms of energy," he said. "Positive or negative?"

"Think positively!" I said, giggling. "Positive, of course!"

Then Uschi chucked us off the stage. "Get down now, you **turtledoves**! We want to start!"

I looked across at her in alarm. Oh my goodness, pretty much everyone from the kissing club was there, looking at Bastian and me.

Surely they hadn't been listening to our whole conversation? They had! When I caught a look from Meik, all doubt was removed. How mega-embarrassing! Earth, open up!

---

roguish – schelmisch;
to chat sb up – jmdn. anmachen;
to disable the laws of gravity – die Gravitationsgesetze außer Kraft setzen; repulsion – Abstoßung;
grey matter – graue Zellen;
turtledove – Turteltaube

Franzi and the Pepper Dollies, however, just found the whole thing exciting and, of course, immediately wanted to know what was suddenly **brewing up** between Bastian and me.

"Nothing," I played it down.

And that was true, too. He'd sent Mona a love-poem, not me. But on the other hand ...

And feeling bold after this successful start, I added, "But if it's nothing now, that doesn't mean it can't become something."

At any rate, he knew now that I fancied him. Wait and see how he'd react to that one.

When we played the next scene together it was clear that he at least didn't hold the embarrassing party catastrophe against me.

"Are you always so dangerous to the public when you've got your eye on a boy?" he asked in a whisper before begging a kiss from me as Petruchio: *"Come on, kiss me Kate."*

I shook my head. "It was a heavenly power," I whispered back and said loudly, *"What, in the midst of the street?"*

Was I mistaken, or did Fabian, who was standing at the edge of the stage, **jump** at these words? He was presumably being plagued by guilt.

Bastian grinned cheekily and you could see that he was obviously enjoying the role. *"Is not this well?*

---

to brew up – *hier:* köcheln;
to jump – *hier:* zusammenzucken

Come, my sweet Kate; Better once than never, for never too late ..."

And as he pulled me into his arms for a stage kiss, he asked quietly, "Do you want to? Or not?"

Out of the corner of my eye I could see Meik and Mona standing next to one another, looking at us in fascination. Then something got into me and I suddenly breathed, "I do want to."

His lips found mine. The touch was strange, but a promising start.

"Thanks," said Uschi, "that was very nice. But drop the whispering in between."

We let go of one another.

I felt the blood rush to my cheeks. *A thousand times touched, a thousand times nothing happened* ... But it was all different today.

What had Mum said? There were people who suddenly fascinate you so much that you're absolutely desperate to get together with them ...

All of a sudden, I felt certain that Bastian was one of those people ...

"What's going on between you two?" Greetje asked at lunch break, and Franzi and Lea, of course, wanted to know more as well.

I gave them a rough outline of the birthday party.

"Stick with it," advised Franzi. "I think he's a totally cool guy. Meik's eyes didn't half pop out of his head. It can't hurt for him to realize that you're not dependent on him."

In Wolfie's Geography lesson, I did suddenly feel really ill, and as I looked it, too, he sent me home.

I went straight to bed and immediately fell asleep, completely exhausted. My God, surely that couldn't just be the after-effects of the alcohol?

When I woke up again, **dusk** was already falling. As I felt incredibly **worn out**, I boiled some water and made myself a dreamy cup of instant coffee. Then I **slunk** into the living room and flopped down on the sofa. I immediately drank a couple of sips of my dreamy coffee, shut my eyes and awaited the dreams that it was supposed to produce.

Somewhere over the rainbow … there's a land that I dreamed of once in a ***lullaby*** *…*

Nothing! Dreamy coffee my foot! A complete **swizz**! Great dreams didn't simply appear. Instead, I suddenly saw Meik's arm before me, lying on Mona's sleeping bag in the 'hay-hotel'. What had happened to our love? I had, in fact, felt a bit sorry for him this morning, but the situation was ultimately his own fault.

My head ached and I pushed aside all thoughts of Meik. Much too depressing. Bastian was a real ray of hope in my currently rather **gloomy** life. He really was more than a **stop-gap**. He was seriously cool!

And I regretted enormously the fact that Uschi had disturbed our kiss much too soon! Plenty of kisses,

---

dusk – Abenddämmerung;
worn out – erschöpft; to slink – schleichen;
lullaby – Schlaflied;
swizz – Schwindel;
gloomy – düster;
stop-gap – Lückenbüßer

plenty of friends! And with an inner giggle, I thought I'd love to know what he tastes like.

That evening I did in fact have a temperature. 38.9. Reason enough for Mum to drag me off to the doctor's the next morning. My **tonsils** were swollen and I felt worn out and wretched.

Our **GP** examined me thoroughly, establishing in the process that my **lymph glands** were distinctly swollen.

"Hmm," he said, looking at me intently. "How old are you now?"

"Thirteen," I replied, wondering what on earth that had to do with my illness.

"I see," he murmured, then he sent Mum out of the consulting room to ask at Reception whether the **ultrasound** room was free.

Barely was she outside when he bent down to me with a **conspiratorial** grin and said, "Are you doing a lot of snogging at the moment?"

The question was completely unexpected and I stammered, confused: "Erm, no, erm, I mean, well yes, but not at the moment, because, it's recently been banned at our school you see ..."

"Recently? How recently? Two, three weeks?"

I nodded. "Yes, about that long."

---

tonsil – Mandel;
GP = General Practioner – Hausarzt;
lymph gland – Lymphdrüse;
ultra-sound – Ultraschall;
conspiratorial – verschwörerisch

"And what about before that? Tried it out a bit with the boys? Have you got a boyfriend?"

Yet more complicated and, what's more, indiscreet questions.

"No, I mean yes, well, not really at the moment ..."

God, what must he think of me. Presumably that my illness was all in my mind.

"Hmm," he said, "I need to do an ultra-sound **scan** and a blood test, but the way it looks, I'd say it was a pretty clear case to me."

But that sounded terrible. And so I asked hesitantly, "Is it – is it something serious?"

He laughed encouragingly. "Serious, yes, because it can be a lengthy business. It's a **viral** illness that's normally **benign** and runs its course. It's caused by the Eppstein-Barr virus. It's transmitted via **droplet infection**."

I stared at him, not understanding a word. So what was the matter with me?

"The kissing **disease**," he said, "so-called **Pfeiffer's glandular fever**. A common illness among young people, which is mainly passed on by kissing."

I thought I was going mad. Surely he had to be joking.

But he wasn't. There really was such a thing as this illness and I had it, quite badly. And the worst thing was

---

scan – *hier:* Aufnahme;
viral – Virus-; benign – gutartig;
droplet infection – Tröpfcheninfektion;
disease – Krankheit;
Pfeiffer's glandular fever – Pfeiffer'sches Drüsenfieber

that there wasn't much you could do about it other than lie in bed like a good girl and leave the rest to the body's own natural defences.

When Franzi rang me that afternoon, she couldn't believe it either. "Kissing disease! I don't believe it. And it really is passed on through **saliva**? Do you think Meik infected you?"

"Who else? The doctor said it normally takes between two and three weeks, sometimes longer, for the illness to start. And after all, I was only with Meik then!"

"But where did he get the virus?" Franzi kept on at me. "Has he been snogging other girls?"

Given my state, that was rather too tactless a question, and so I answered rather nastily, "Well, I don't know!"

She saw her mistake and immediately said apologetically, "Presumably, you can also get it if you drink out of the same bottle as someone else, can't you?"

"What do I know," I said, exhausted. "I don't care either. At any rate, I can't go to school for at least two weeks. You'll have to excuse me with all the teachers."

"Will do, will do. Should I let Meik know, too?"

"No," I refused her offer. "I'll tell him myself." And to myself, I thought: if he ever gets in touch with me again.

He got in touch the very next day, and I was sure that Franzi had said something to him. I was glad, but at the same time I wasn't glad. Oh, it was all so dead-end and

---

saliva – Spucke

I felt too worn out to discuss our difficult relationship with him.

So I quickly hung up on him with a **lame** excuse about tiredness and said that I'd be in touch when I felt better. But I didn't have the courage. And so it happened that we didn't hear from one another for two whole weeks.

If I hadn't had videos to watch, I'd have gone mad with boredom. But when all was said and done, I couldn't spend the whole time **goggling at the box**. I was already getting square eyes.

So I rang Franzi. "I'm talking to the sofa, flirting with the TV and the video recorder, breakfasting with the toaster and I'm about to start having an affair with the vacuum cleaner. I'll go mad if you don't come to visit me soon!"

"So aren't you **contagious** any more?"

"No! I'm not! And anyway, I'm not an **elk** and I've got no intention of trying to snog you either!"

Franzi **called in** remorsefully straight after school.

She offloaded a gigantic mountain of girls' and women's magazines onto my sofa and said apologetically, "I really didn't want to neglect you, but Meik said you couldn't have visitors."

So that's what he said. **Prat**. Not wanting to see him

---

lame – lahm;
to goggle at the box – Fernsehen glotzen;
contagious – ansteckend; elk – Elch;
to call in – vorbeikommen;
prat – Dummkopf

didn't mean that I didn't want to see my friends. What did it have to do with him anyway?

Once Franzi had gone, I took the magazines and **brooded over** dozens of relationship tests as to why Meik **allegedly** suited me so well and yet it still hadn't worked out.

So far as Bastian was concerned, he was still writing M-lieschen enthusiastic e-mails, which led me to think that he for one was pretty keen on Mona.

I sighed. Mona, always Mona. She was always in my way.

I stared angrily at the last e-mail that I'd written as M-lieschen. What on earth possessed me, pairing off such a great guy as Bastian with Mona? Just because of that stupid bet with Franzi? Surely not.

It was time for me to stop hiding behind this secret address. I finally had to open Bastian's eyes as to M-lieschen's real identity. And this seemed to me to be a pretty good moment. He wasn't angry with me any more; he'd even flirted with me and if Uschi hadn't disturbed us … who knows what that stage kiss might have turned into?

Even if I didn't go around **flaunting** such a great backside as Mona's, maybe he could fall in love with me after all. Perhaps his heart and head also had a say – and

---

to brood over sth – über etwas brüten;
alleged – angeblich;
to flaunt – zur Schau stellen

he had plenty of both. And what's more, I was just as romantic as him!

With every e-mail that we exchanged, however, I just sent him further into Mona's arms.

So what does that tell us? asked my inner coach. Precisely! That I had to put a stop to this M-lieschen business. But I'd have to talk to him in order to do so. There's no way I could ever do that; I immediately erased the thought from my mind.

But why? said the inner voice.

I couldn't look him in the eye; I would sink into the ground with embarrassment.

*Do you have to meet him **in the flesh**?*

How else? Now I really didn't get it.

Well, virtually. Just arrange to meet him in a chat room!

I could have snogged my inner coach. That was a brilliant idea. And my fingers were already rushing across the keys.

I named a private chat room which I'd once set up with Franzi, and invited him for a chat at nine o'clock.

Seriously worked up, I sat at my computer that evening. I'd already said goodnight to Mum and The Joker, and could be sure that nobody would disturb me again.

Would he really come?

I entered the lobby.

There are two people in the chat room.

---

in the flesh – leibhaftig

He was there.

Hello, Bastinochild!

Hello, Monalieschen!

Oh, now it really was clear that he thought I was Mona. What a pity!

Why are you here?

I'd like to be your boyfriend.

Hello, I knew this dialogue. It came from the film *You've Got Mail*. How did it carry on? Think, think.

You hardly know me, and yet you so often write that you love me. What if I were totally different from what you thought?

I somehow had to let him know that I, Kiki, was the one who was writing these e-mails, not Mona.

:-)) It is as it is! I love you the way you are. I see you before me and know it's you, my Monalieschen – let's stop playing this game of hide and seek.

Oh God! Not that! All of a sudden it was clear to me that I needed a lot more time to spell it out to him very carefully that there was **a case of mistaken identity** going on and that he didn't really love Mona but Monalieschen, and that meant – me.

I hurriedly left the chat room.

I couldn't sleep. The problem seemed much worse than I'd thought. My God, how I **envied** Mona. What wouldn't I give to get such lovely e-mails from a boy!

When I felt a bit better, I decided to put a stop to all

---

a case of mistaken identity – eine Verwechslung;
to envy – beneiden

the e-mailing with Bastian. It really was unbearable that on top of everything else, I should **fire up** Bastian's **besottedness** or even love for Mona. Logic told me that my messages were doing precisely that. He was totally fixated. If I wanted to win him over, I'd have to do it another way. And so from one day to the next, I stopped e-mailing Bastian. He wrote three more times, but as I didn't reply, he got in touch one final time, and then there was silence:

Why doesn't my song penetrate your ear?
Is the wind too loud these days?
Should I fetch the trumpets
so that the sound carries further?
Oh, don't tell me it's no good,
my love is with you everywhere,
I can never be away from you,
but you've not the faintest idea about it!

Although it was somehow sad, I had to laugh. How well Bastian with his absurd humour would have gone together with Mona! But it was obvious that for some reason or another, things hadn't really **taken off** for them after the party. And I was sure that it was to do with Meik. Meik, whom Mona would undoubtedly have thrown herself at now that I was ill, and who wasn't getting in touch with me because of her. The **mere** thought of it kept **dragging me down**.

---

to fire up – anheizen;
besottedness – Schwärmerei;
to take off – *hier:* losgehen, anfangen; mere – bloß;
to drag sb down – herunterziehen

And so I didn't just have the kissing disease but was **lovesick** as well, and in many feverish dreams I gradually came to rid myself of the hope of ever getting back together with Meik.

Of course I **sounded** Franzi **out** about Meik, Mona and Bastian every time she visited, but she evidently didn't want to worry me, and just kept reporting **trivia**. And so I was happy when the doctor finally gave me the green light and allowed me to go back to school.

I immediately noticed that things had moved on. For some **unfathomable** reason word had got around about my illness and I had to put up with all kinds of stupid comments.

Even Wolfie had the **effrontery** to misuse my kissing illness as an argument in favour of Frau Biedermann's kissing ban.

"If you'd stuck to her rules, you'd not have got this disease," he said rather unsympathetically.

And the Slugs mocked thereupon, "Ha, she who won't listen has to feel it ..."

I, however, **gave them the brush-off** by saying, "Well, at least I'm one hundred percent immune, so I can snog whoever I like as much as I like! Ha ha!"

Well, I could if I had anyone, I thought, for I had com-

---

to be lovesick – Liebeskummer haben;
to sound sb out – jmdn. ausfragen;
trivia – Belanglosigkeiten; unfathomable – unergründlich;
effrontery – Frechheit;
to give sb the brush-off – jmdn. abblitzen lassen

pletely written Meik off. When I passed his table at lunch, he quickly looked down at his plate as if he didn't want to have to see me. So that was the end of my first love! I bit my lower lip.

The bell had long since rung, and we were waiting for Wolfie again. Since the class trip, he'd been constantly hanging out with Biedermann in her office, and kept being late for class. Great! **Plaguing** us with every possible order whilst shortening our teaching time himself! What on earth did he get up to in there with Biedermann?

"I think he **worships** her," said Lea. What a romantic soul!

"Rubbish," said Franzi. "He's acting head. They must just have all kinds of things to discuss."

At that moment the door banged behind Wolfie. "Sorry," he said. "An urgent work conversation …" And as he spoke, his whole head turned red.

"Really?" said Mona. "Should the kissing ban be lifted, perhaps?"

Wolfie looked at her disapprovingly. "I had to sign the contract for the school uniforms."

"No!"

"In two weeks, they're delivering the **samples**." With an insinuating look at Mona and me, he added, "And we have two experienced models in our class. You can model them for the students' assembly!"

He couldn't be serious!

---

to plague sb – jmdn. plagen; to worship – anhimmeln;
sample – Muster

When I went to the music room with the Pepper Dollies, Franzi took me aside and said, "Now, don't have a fit, Kiki. It'll all be sorted out calmly."

"What will be sorted out calmly?" I asked, highly anxious.

"The business about the roles. But prepare yourself for a shock first."

I had a **sense of foreboding**, but then it really did hit me like a hammer blow. The **scales** fell from my eyes and I now understood why Meik hadn't got in touch again and had seemed so **buttoned up** at lunchtime.

I grabbed Franzi's hand. "Hold on to me," I hissed at her, "or I'll act like a woman **possessed**!"

"Calm, calm," she warned me, but held my hand tightly.

Mona must have taken complete advantage of my illness to suck right up to Uschi. At any rate, she was suddenly playing all my roles and was lying alternately in the arms of Meik and Bastian. I was simultaneously angry and at a loss. Couldn't anyone see what kind of ego-fest was going off on stage?

"Why are we actually here?" I asked Franzi, totally furious. "*We* were the ones who came up with the idea in the first place, and now we're supposed to be bystanders for Mona and her admirers! Nobody's going to do that to me!"

And before Franzi could stop me, I stormed onto the

---

sense of foreboding – Vorahnung;
scale – Schuppe; to be buttoned up – zugeknöpft sein;
possessed – besessen

stage where Bastian and Mona were just sinking with the Titanic. I **shoved Mona aside** and yelled more than spoke to Uschi, "That was my scene! I'm more than in a position to play it again. Mona really doesn't have to do everything!"

Mona looked at me in astonishment. "But you've never been here! Someone had to stand in for you, and I simply offered."

"Well, thanks a lot! But I can do it myself again now!"

"Fine," Mona **pacified** me. "I was only interested in our cause. Nobody knew when you were going to be fit again, and the revue is, after all, supposed to be part of the summer party." And turning to Uschi, she added, "If Kiki's joining in again, she's very welcome to have her parts back. I really don't want to **impose**."

She made an inviting gesture to Bastian, who was leaning against the improvised rail of the Titanic and had watched our quarrel with amusement.

"Here, your doom awaits you!" she said with a cool grin. The girl was simply unbeatable.

"Well, then!" said Uschi. "Look sharp, get started. Bastian, give Kiki her **cue**."

I went over to Bastian. He gave me a rather strange look, and I was totally **gripped by** the panic on the Ti-

---

to shove sb aside – jmdn. beiseiteschieben;
to pacify sb – jmdn. beruhigen;
to impose – sich aufdrängen;
cue – Stichwort;
to be gripped by sth – von etwas erfasst sein

tanic. I was on the point of running off the stage and leaving the field open for Mona of my own free will, when I suddenly realised that a wonderful opportunity was presenting itself to me. And in a fit of **defiance** and fearlessness in the face of death, I threw myself into Bastian's arms and pressed my lips to his mouth. He was initially caught completely unawares, but then he held me tightly, pressed me to him, and began to return my kiss. Hesitantly and **tentatively** at first, then unashamedly and provocatively. One thing was immediately clear to me: the boy was no beginner. He really could kiss! Wow!

Around me sank the Titanic, the school, the world, the universe. At some point, loud applause tore me from my **oblivion**.

Breathlessly, we let one another go. I stared into the laughing faces of the Pepper Dollies and the rather **distressed** face of Uschi.

Van Gogh was **beaming**. "I said so. You're an ideal couple."

Whether he meant on stage or in real life wasn't clear.

Even Mona forced herself to grin in an heroic gesture, but said rather **pointedly**, "I thought this was all about acting and not about the private lives of the ac-

---

defiance – Trotz;
tentative – vorsichtig;
oblivion – Vergessenheit;
distressed – *hier:* verstört;
to beam – strahlen; pointed – spitz

tors, but hey, if the pair of them are having so much fun showing off in public ..."

With that, she quickly left the music room. Hello, I thought, that presumably didn't suit her.

After we'd rehearsed all our scenes I was about to go back to our classroom with Franzi when I felt Meik's hand on my arm.

I turned to him and looked directly into his blue eyes. It was incredible how much I'd missed them!

"Are you free after school?" he asked.

Hmm, was I? Should I be? Nah, better not. He surely just wanted to test how serious it was between Bastian and me. No doubt he couldn't bear to see me in another boy's arms. Well, now he could see for himself what a horrible feeling it was! No, he shouldn't get the idea that I'd immediately come trotting along when he whistled. I shook my head. "Nah, it really isn't **convenient** today. I was going with Basti..." I put my hand up to my mouth as if I'd let the cat out of the bag.

"Pity," said Meik. "I think we should talk ..."

Yes, I thought, we really should talk. But I just shrugged my shoulders and said coolly, "Sorry, maybe another time."

And as Bastian passed us, I slipped my arm into his, as Mona always did, and said provocatively, "I could sink on the Titanic every day with you!"

---

convenient – passend

The Pepper Dollies were, of course, flabbergasted. And on the way home on the bus, they immediately wanted to know whether van Gogh was right and Bastian and I were now a couple.

I just shook my head meaningfully. To be honest, I didn't know either. But I could certainly imagine it. And when I got a sweet text from him that evening, I was happy again for the first time in ages.

Suddenly **fortune** smiled upon me.

When I got to school a bit late the next day on account of the bus breaking down, the Pepper Dollies were awaiting me with sensational news.

"Mona's ill!" bubbled Franzi as I went to my seat.

"Quiet please!" grumbled Frau Ingrimm. "If you're late, Kiki, then at least show some consideration."

"I am, but I can't help it if the bus is late." I sat down.

"What's the matter with her?" I asked Franzi in a whisper.

"Brace yourself: the kissing disease!"

At the rehearsals Mona's illness **plunged** everyone into **paralytic** horror, as it was clear that there was no way she'd be fit for the summer party. Uschi and van Gogh were completely shattered and considered every possible casting alternative.

We finally reached a compromise. Greetje, who could

---

fortune – Glück;
to plunge into – stürzen in;
paralytic – lähmend

sing pretty well, took over a share of Mona's songs, and I stepped in for the acting scenes. This meant that I constantly had to change costume at breakneck speed. Good job I'd **devised** a particular quick-change routine for the fashion show. Otherwise, the whole thing would have failed – guaranteed.

I was at least spared Mona's ape costume because Lea offered to play the feeding ape-mother for the Gorillas, and Raffi and Franzi, once again one heart and one soul, volunteered to eat spaghetti together for *Lady And The Tramp*.

"Good," said van Gogh. "If we're all agreed, then we'll risk these re-castings."

Then events came thick and fast. The summer party was right upon us, and the dress rehearsal was fixed for the kissing revue. We'd done the first part with anecdotes and poems and now it was just the film scenes that were waiting to be dealt with. Uschi sat at the piano and Greetje sang *A kiss is just a kiss* from *Casablanca*.

I had the feeling that I was coming into ever better form without Mona breathing down my neck, and more than once saw the admiration sparkling in Meik's eyes. And then it happened. After consulting Uschi, I'd learnt Mona's part for the final scene of *You've Got Mail*, the one between Tom Hanks and Meg Ryan, and now I was to perform it for the first time with Meik.

---

to devise – *hier:* sich aneignen

"If you do it well," said Uschi, "we'll still include it. If not, then we'll just have to ditch it."

We took our places. In the background, Greetje sang in her lovely, clear voice, accompanied by the jazz combo, *Somewhere Over The Rainbow.*

"... where ***sorrows*** *melt like lemon drops ... that's where you'll find me ..."*

My knees suddenly turned wobbly because it all of a sudden occurred to me that it had been precisely this film that Meik and I had seen on our first cinema date. I had felt like a **squidgy** pink marshmallow and I'd forgotten everything around me as he began to nibble at me. God, why did I have to remember that now? Meik's voice suddenly penetrated my consciousness as if through soft cotton wool.

"Don't cry," he said, sounding almost like Tom Hanks. *"Don't cry."*

Two tears suddenly rolled from my eyes. With a gentle hand movement he wiped them away.

Sniffing, I stuck my nose up just as Meg Ryan had done. *"I so much wanted it to be you ..."* I **quoted from** the film text, my voice failing. Oh God, what on earth was going to happen next?

Then Meik just took me in his arms without saying a single unnecessary word more and kissed me.

And I suddenly knew that things aren't always the way they appear to be, and I realised that everything I'd

---

sorrow – Sorge;
squidgy – durchweicht;
to quote from – zitieren aus

thought and feared was wrong. Here in Meik's arms and in his kiss lay the whole and only truth.

"Somewhere over the rainbow skiers are blue and the dreams that you dare to dream really do come true …"

When Meik asked me after the rehearsal that day if I had time to talk after school, I said yes.

"Okay, do you want to come to mine? I'll cook you spaghetti."

Who could resist such an offer? Not me, at any rate.

Lea and Franzi cast me meaningful looks when I got onto the bus with Meik that afternoon, and when we got off the bus, they called after me, "Have a nice evening, and remember not to start too much snogging again too soon!"

I must be driving them crazy! First Bastian, then Meik again! But the business wasn't over yet. Everything would depend on this conversation. I was **intrigued** to see how he'd talk his way out of it.

At the supermarket on the corner we bought spaghetti, tomato puree and **minced beef**.

"Shall I make a salad to go with it?" I let myself get carried away into offering a service.

"If you like. But you'll have to do it on your own. I don't know anything about salad."

Well, we **complemented each other** fantastically: I

---

to be intrigued – neugierig sein;
minced beef – Rinderhack;
to complement each other – sich ergänzen

was a lousy cook and at best only useful for serving up cold dishes.

So I put a mixed salad into the shopping trolley along with the brilliant Italian packet sauce.

Nothing could go wrong.

Your kisses belong only to me

Shortly afterwards I entered Meik's flat for the first time.

He lived with his mother on the **attic floor** of a **terraced house** that belonged to his grandparents. It was light and **handsomely** renovated with lots of wood and parquet floors, and I immediately found it very cosy.

"The house had become too big for my grandparents on their own." He put our shopping onto the breakfast bar in the small but well **equipped** kitchen.

"What about your father? Are your parents separated?"

He nodded. "Yes. Two years ago. It sounds stupid, but I was quite glad about it. Finally the end of the constant rows. You never really know who's right, and you don't want to take sides. So it was good that my father took a job abroad. Maybe ... if he ever comes back ... who knows ... maybe they'll get on better ..."

---

attic floor – Dachgeschoss;
terraced house – Reihenhaus;
handsome – großzügig; equipped – ausgestattet

I nodded. "It may well be. A temporary separation is sometimes quite good. It often makes your thoughts and feelings clearer."

Meik gave me a penetrating look. "Which takes us straight to the point, even if we're not even onto the **first course** yet."

"True. When I was ill, I really had a lot of time to think."

He put the water on for the spaghetti and started to prepare the sauce in a little saucepan while I washed the salad.

"Well? What was the result of your thinking? Why did everything suddenly go so wrong between us?" He poked around at the **sizzling** minced beef.

"You know better than anyone. What was going on between you and Mona in the 'hay-hotel'?"

Meik stopped stirring and looked at me in astonishment. "In the 'hay-hotel'? Between Mona and me?"

"Don't act so innocent," I retorted, the very thought of it making me angry again. "Why was your arm lying on her sleeping bag?"

"My arm? On Mona's sleeping bag?" He shook his head in bewilderment as if he couldn't begin to comprehend what I'd just said. "I've got no idea what you're talking about."

He was either a good actor or he really did have no idea. I was almost inclined to believe the latter, because

---

first course – erster Gang, Vorspeise;
to sizzle – brutzeln

he was looking at me truly uncomprehendingly out of his blue eyes.

"But your arm was on her sleeping bag in the morning, and it looked as if you'd spent the whole night **cuddled up to** her!"

My voice must have sounded pretty **agitated** because he took the pan off the stove and came over to me and put his arm around my shoulders.

"But that's complete nonsense! Why should I have been cuddled up to Mona? We were a couple at that time, you and me. The business with the arm must have been pure coincidence. We were lying all jumbled up in the hay, weren't we? Really, I didn't have the slightest interest in Mona then!"

"So, not then. But today? What about now? Is something going on between you? Everybody says so!"

He turned me round so that he could look into my eyes. "So, everyone! Who's everyone? The Pepper Dollies or even the Slugs?"

"For example!"

"You surely don't believe them!"

"Why not? Are they wrong? Tell me, are they really wrong? Did nothing go on between you and Mona when I was ill?"

I wanted to know precisely now! If we were getting things off our chests, then let's do it properly. Then everything had to be on the table, not just the spaghetti!

---

to cuddle up to sb – sich an jmdn. kuscheln;
agitated – erregt

Meik lowered his eyes. Aha, so I was right! My suspicions were correct.

"It's not what you think ..." he began.

Oh no, so what did I think? That he'd been snogging Mona?

"I ... well, you were so cold after the trip to the 'hay-hotel', now I know why, but I had no idea then ... and when you were ill and didn't want me to visit you, then I thought that you didn't want to know about me any more ..."

"And then along came Mona, **conveniently** enough, and consoled you!"

I noticed how my anger with Mona was rising within me again.

"We acted out so many love-scenes together and then it just happened ... I didn't want it to ... it was really more acting than reality ..."

"Like with us today?"

"Oh, Kiki, don't make it so difficult for me! You know full well that it wasn't like that! Do you really think I could kiss another girl like I kiss you?"

"No? You couldn't? Why not?" What was different with me from with Mona? Now that did interest me.

He went back to the stove, stirred the spaghetti in the boiling water and put the saucepan back on the heat. As he stirred vigorously, I could almost feel physically the way he was struggling for words.

"Mona is an exciting and very pretty girl!" it sud-

---

convenient – *hier:* bequem

denly burst out of him. "But I'd never have a relationship with her! My nerves couldn't take it!"

I had to laugh, and I was reminded of Mum's words about how you sometimes meet people you find fascinating for a while, but whom you'd never have a lasting intimate relationship with. Mona was such a fascinating and undoubtedly likeable person, but she wasn't real competition for me. Meik had briefly **succumbed to** her charms, but he didn't want her as his girlfriend – he wanted me.

"So you think you could stand it better with me than with her?" I said after thinking these thoughts. "Aren't I too **stroppy** for you?"

He turned and looked me straight in the face. "Yes, sometimes," he said with a laugh. "But then you're a girl!"

"**Caveman**!" I cried in mock anger, and threw the kitchen towel at him.

He caught it and used it to take the spaghetti pan off the stove and **drain** the spaghetti. "Hey, make room! Isn't your salad clean enough yet?" He shoved me away from the sink.

I took the lettuce, which had collapsed somewhat in the meantime, and threw it into a bowl together with the dressing.

"Time to eat now," said Meik decisively, "we can carry on **poring over** our problems afterwards!"

---

to succumb to sth/sb – etwas/jmdm. erliegen;
stroppy – widerspenstig; caveman – *hier:* Macho;
to drain – abgießen; to pore over – grübeln über

The salad was **mushy,** as was the spaghetti, and the sauce was a bit burnt, but for me it was the best meal I'd had in ages. Better than nectar and ambrosia, the food of the gods.

Later we sat in Meik's room on a **pile** of colourful mattresses and listened to CDs. I put my head on his shoulder and he stroked my arm.

"Is everything okay again?" he asked.

I snuggled up to him and thought about Mum's words about the importance of **mutual** freedom and trust for a lasting relationship.

Why shouldn't something that had worked for my parents for 15 years not work for me, too?

"When Bastian kissed you on stage in front of everyone, I thought I couldn't stand it. I'd have loved to have torn him away from you." Meik was silent for a serious moment. "Then it was suddenly clear that I wanted you back. At all costs!"

Now I presumably had some explaining to do as well. "Erm, so far as Bastian's concerned …"

"Yes?"

"Well, I think I just wanted to use him to make you jealous at first, but if we hadn't **made up**, who knows … He's at least as attractive to me as Mona was to you."

"He *was* as attractive," Meik corrected me. "After all, we're together now, aren't we?"

"When opportunity knocks …," I teased him, but

---

mushy – matschig; pile – Stapel; mutual – gegenseitig; to make up – sich versöhnen then added **peaceably,** "okay, fine, we're quits. I think I can trust you." And after thinking for a short while, I repeated it again as if to reassure myself as well: "Yes, I think I really can trust you. And you can trust me, too."

There was still one small problem: Bastian. He was too nice for me to play with. I had to tell him the truth as quickly as possible. Hmm, I thought, maybe I can sweeten the bitter pill for him somewhat.

Uschi had arranged another dress rehearsal **at quite short notice** and as I stood before Bastian all beautifully dressed up, he, of course, wanted to take advantage of his role again in order to snog me. If Frau Biedermann had had the faintest idea of what was going on under her school roof, she'd have **gone ballistic**.

Bastian pulled me to him, but I plucked up my courage and wriggled away discreetly but clearly. No more beating about the bush!

"Sorry, I'm back together with Meik now," I said quietly to him. "That means it's just film kisses for us from now on. But maybe you should try Mona when she's better."

And as he stared at me, kind of bemused, I added **craftily**, "You should send her such mega-sweet e-mails. I think she's mad about you."

As his eyes lit up at these words, I spontaneously decided to grab the bull by the horns. If it hadn't worked

---

peaceable – friedfertig;
at quite short notice – ziemlich kurzfristig;
to go ballistic – an die Decke gehen; crafty – listig

first time, then it didn't mean that my idea of pairing Mona and Bastian off was a bad one. At the end of the day, she was the one he'd really fallen for, and I reckoned that they kind of went together brilliantly. It was at least worth a second try. And didn't I still have an outstanding bet with Franzi?

After school I got on the bus with Meik. Franzi and Lea weren't the only ones who were surprised. Even Meik asked, "Hey, are you coming to mine again?"

I shook my head. "Not today. I'm going to Mona's."

Great astonishment.

"To Mona's?" Franzi didn't remotely get it. "But why?"

"I just feel sorry for her. She was so looking forward to the revue, and now it's starting without her on Saturday. Just because of that stupid kissing disease. Believe me, I know what she's going through."

It seemed to me that all three of them were looking at me with a certain degree of astonishment. Yes, siree, Kiki can be generous, too!

Mona was, of course, perplexed. No doubt I was the very last person she'd expected to see when she opened her front door.

She let me in and led me through an elegant hallway to her room.

Very Mona, I thought, completely modish. Gigantic photos of the modelling competition **adorned** the walls

---

to adorn – zieren

alongside posters of Che Guevara and the No Angels. In between were romantic images of the rain forest and Caribbean palm beaches. A **chunky** Nana statue was enthroned on top of the television.

"Sit down," said Mona, gesticulating towards a brightly-coloured cocktail chair. "Do you want a drink?"

"I wouldn't mind some water."

When she returned with it, I asked, "How's your throat? Does it still hurt like mad?"

"It's okay. I'm getting cortisone now. My **spleen's** a bit swollen, and so's my **liver**. I'd never have thought that this stupid kissing disease could take it out of you to such an extent. Do you think Meik infected us?"

I started. She couldn't admit more clearly that she'd had something going with him! But before I could become really angry about it, she noticed herself what she'd gone and done yet again in her rash way.

"Oh, Kiki," she said, sounding genuinely **dismayed**. "I'm sorry! I honestly only kissed him once ... he ... he ... seemed so sad and I thought it was over between you two ..."

Okay, that could actually correspond to reality; it did, at any rate, agree with what Meik told me.

"I'd never **pinch** your boyfriend!"

Hmm, should I buy that one?

"You know me. I like flirting, but my friends' boyfriends are absolutely taboo for me!"

---

chunky – fett; spleen – Milz; liver – Leber;
dismayed – bestürzt; to pinch – *hier:* ausspannen

Okay, okay, I believed her!

"So we're friends then. Aren't we?"

I nodded resignedly. Why should I complicate matters unnecessarily?

"Tell me about the revue," she said, changing the subject abruptly and suddenly looking really sad.

"Bastian says hello," I said in order to cheer her up a bit.

"Oh yes?"

"So why didn't you become a couple after his party?" I asked. "You seemed very much in love with one another then ..."

Mona seemed to ponder for a moment. "True. He was totally sweet, invited me completely spontaneously, and he wasn't a bad kisser either ..."

She banged her forehead with her hand.

"How long does it take for this kissing disease to start?"

"Two to three weeks, sometimes five to seven ..."

"Do you think I could have been infected at Bastian's party?"

The idea wasn't unpleasant to me. At any rate, I much preferred it to the version which had Meik as the source of infection.

I grinned cheekily. "You know better than anyone."

I pulled myself together as it seemed a good moment. "By the way, I think Bastian's pretty keen on you."

She seemed disbelieving. "I've thought he's been very cool recently."

Of course I could understand that, when Monalieschen had all of a sudden stopped replying to his e-mails. But how could I do something about it? "Have you got a computer with an Internet connection?"

She had.

"May I use it for a moment?"

Astonishment. But she stood up to switch the PC on.

"Go to the Internet. Okay, then let me do it. I want to show you something." I went to my Monalieschen mailbox.

Hello M-lieschen, you've got new mail.

Mona looked at the name with irritation. "M-lieschen?"

I giggled nervously, as I was totally **on edge**. "Comes from Monalisa," I explained.

Now she seemed seriously mistrustful. "Why have you got yourself an alias? It sounds more like me."

"It's supposed to," I ventured a first hint. "I set up this mailbox for you, you see ..." And before Mona could **blow her top**, I added, "... to pair you off with Bastian! So that you'd keep your hands off Meik! Please don't yell at me and chuck me out! Instead, read what Bastian wrote to you. I've saved it all!"

Mona was silent with complete astonishment. What I'd just **revealed** to her no doubt **surpassed** even her imagination.

But she then said in a flash of inspiration, "At some point during his party, Bastian kept calling me Mona-lieschen. I found it pretty annoying, especially all the

---

to be on edge – hibbelig sein;
to blow one's top – hochgehen;
to reveal – enthüllen; to surpass – übersteigen

strange allusions that I didn't remotely understand ... Now of course I'm beginning to get it ..."

It was certainly a rather schizophrenic situation, but funny, surely.

I grinned inwardly and went to the most recent e-mail. It was bound to be from Bastian, and I was curious myself to see what he might have written after I'd given him new hopes with regard to Mona that morning.

The e-mail was indeed from him.

Monalieschen, get better soon and write to me again! I still love you!
Bastian

I was triumphant. "See, did I promise too much? The boy really is nuts about you!"

For the first time since I'd known Mona, she was completely at a loss. I took a pen from her desk and wrote the password down for her.

"Aphrodite?"

"Yes. Goddess of love seemed very appropriate to me. But you should change the password. After all, it's your flirting address for Bastian from now on, and I'm sure you don't want me **snooping around** after you, should **temptation** overcome me. His e-mails really are mega-sweet, you see!" I sighed.

Mona looked at me sceptically. "Why aren't you starting anything with him?"

---

to snoop around – herumschnüffeln;
temptation – Versuchung

"No chance," I admitted honestly. "He did try to nibble me again today at the rehearsal, but I'd say it was just out of desperation. I'm the bird in the hand for him. But you're the two in the bush. Just get out of it."

I stood up.

"Don't let the poor boy stew for too long," I advised her as we said goodbye at the door.

With the kind of spontaneous gesture that only Mona was capable of, she took me in her arms. "Thanks, Kiki," she said. "I'll never forget what you did. You're a true friend."

Now she really was embarrassing me.

Then it was time for the summer party. All over the school grounds and the hall stage we'd erected the gigantic kissing ban posters that we'd secretly painted in van Gogh's lessons. Frau Biedermann, of course, didn't find it in the slightest bit funny and demanded that they be cleared away before the start of the party. But she was **banging her head against a brick wall** there. None of us was willing to do it, and van Gogh feigned **deafness** to that sort of thing and just murmured something about "artistic freedom." However, when Frau Biedermann then dragged the caretaker along so that he could remove the offending objects, the Art teacher opposed her heroically. "If you touch my works of art, I'll

---

to bang one's head against a brick wall – mit dem Kopf gegen die Wand laufen; deafness – Taubheit

resign," he said, and planted himself, ready for battle, in front of a poster with a big red kissing mouth on it.

"Fantastic, absolutely fantastic!" said a voice behind us. "That's a brilliant shot!" And click: the photographer for the local newspaper had the scene in the can.

The crowds began to flood in, and Frau Biedermann **pursed her lips** and disappeared angrily into her study. Well, hopefully she'd stay there. A **vain** hope.

Of course she'd **rumbled** that something was going on in the hall, and so she appeared there right before the start of the revue. Now we all started to feel rather anxious. But Fabian and his Gorillas were so ape-like in their ape costumes that we **eventually** forgot Frau Biedermann. After the Sioux kissing dance we were all quite relaxed and when we performed a round of ten "Papuas" nose-kisses, the crowd in the hall was yelling. We could hardly suppress our laughter ourselves and from then onwards, it all happened as if of its own accord. We all rose to astonishing form. I changed my costumes with immense haste and felt myself becoming more confident and better from scene to scene.

"Remember that it's just a film kiss," I warned Bastian as I sank into his arms in Mona's place.

He **skilfully** turned me away from the audience and whispered, "Thanks for getting me together with

---

to resign – kündigen;
to purse one's lips – *hier:* die Lippen zusammenkneifen;
vain – vergeblich; to rumble sth – etwas spitzkriegen;
eventual – schließlich;
skilful – geschickt

Mona. How do you fancy opening a dating agency? You seem to have a real talent for it!"

When the scene with Romeo and Juliet then came and Meik kissed me, I felt so transported back to the start of our love that I almost forgot what was going on around me. If Franzi and Raffi hadn't **neatly** pushed us off the stage, we'd presumably have carried on kissing there for hours.

It turned dramatic after the kisses under the school gates when Greetje appeared as Frau Biedermann and drove the kissing couples apart with threatening gestures. Of course the entire hall soon joined in with *Kissing Forbidden*. When all the posters that still remained on the stage had been destroyed, Frau Biedermann turned as white as chalk. Oh, oh, I thought, I bet she's going to choke on her own anger.

The audience, including an enthusiastically clapping Mona, had meanwhile got up off their chairs, and when thunderous applause broke out Frau Biedermann hurriedly left the hall by a side exit.

At the final bow I waved proudly to my parents and Joker, who had fought their way through the **milling crowd** and almost as far as the stage.

Mona came on stage and gave van Gogh and Uschi each a large and truly well-earned bunch of flowers.

Then she slipped away through the stage door with Bastian, admittedly with a **reminder** that she hadn't yet

---

neat – *hier:* elegant; milling crowd – Gewimmel;
reminder – Ermahnung

recovered from her illness. Well, hopefully he really was immune! I could hardly believe that they'd end up not snogging after this thrilling performance.

A guy from the local press interviewed Meik and me, and we told him that we'd rehearsed the revue in secret in order to protest against the undemocratic measures and authoritarian leadership style of Frau Biedermann.

"We used the kissing ban as a **peg** to hang it on," said Meik, "but it is, of course, just a symbol for the totally **retrograde** steps at our school which Frau Biedermann is responsible for. Never was the school climate so lousy!"

On Monday a big article then appeared in the local paper which made rather a joke of our headmistress's measures.

***Swotting** instead of snogging – Pisa bears strange fruit.*

Biedermann was hopping mad and ordered the class reps into the hall. There she complained about the whole action and made it unmistakeably clear, "You can't **lever out** my measures like this. All my orders and particularly the kissing ban on the school premises remain in place!"

"What a **washout**," said Franzi in irritation, casting

---

peg – Aufhänger; retrograde – rückschrittlich;
to swot – büffeln, pauken;
to lever out – aushebeln;
washout – Reinfall

a look at Raffi, who blew her a kiss in return. He was presumably more than ready for a relationship!

We thought and thought, but the Pepper Dollies were at a loss, and the Slugs were triumphant.

That afternoon I went to see Mona to take her a couple of pieces of work so that she didn't lose contact with lessons. She was cross, too, when she heard that all our efforts, the weeks of research and rehearsals, had been **to** absolutely **no avail** and that Frau Biedermann wasn't prepared to make even the slightest concessions.

"I think she's inhuman," I moaned. "At any rate, she's got no heart."

"I wouldn't be so sure," said Mona. "There are certain signs ..." And she suddenly began to grin broadly, as if she'd just had a totally **hilarious** idea. "Hey, isn't there something brewing up between Wolfie and Frau Biedermann? I had the impression that they somehow got close after the canoeing trip. Hasn't he recently been spending his breaks in her office?"

I nodded. "Yes, I've noticed that, too. He's also almost always late for classes, and embarrassed when he gets there."

"Well, I'd love to be a fly on the wall with them," said Mona, giggling. "But since it's not that easy, I suggest ..."

And then she outlined a brilliant plan. If it worked, we were saved.

---

to no avail – vergeblich;
hilarious – witzig

The next morning I let Meik in on it, and together we turned the idea into reality.

He went into the anteroom of the head's office and had her secretary tell her that she was to go most urgently to the library where Dr. Wolf was expecting her.

I **nabbed** Wolfie before the lesson and said, "Frau Biedermann wants you to go quickly to the library. It's really very urgent."

He did an immediate about turn and I crept after him. When he'd disappeared into the library, Meik appeared from behind a pillar in the corridor.

"Is she already in there?" I whispered.

He nodded. "Then let's go for it!"

Cautiously we opened the library door. At first it looked as if the library were empty. But as we crept along the shelves, we could hardly believe our eyes. What we saw **exceeded** our wildest speculations. In a row quite far from the doorway were Frau Biedermann and Wolfie locked in a tight embrace of a quite **unambiguous** nature.

I held the camera up and pressed. The flash popped several times.

The two sinners, caught in the act, jumped apart. Meik grabbed my arm and pulled me out of the library. Just in time, for with a cry of, "Bring that camera back! Bring back the film!" Frau Biedermann rushed after us in a total panic. But she didn't catch us.

---

to nab – abfangen;
to exceed – übertreffen;
unambiguous – unzweideutig

Of course she **summoned** Meik and me to her office later.

"Where's the film?"

"Gone."

"I want the photos!"

Meik grinned cheekily. "You can have them – they're appearing in a special **issue** of the student newspaper tomorrow."

And everyone could in fact see them there. The delight of the pupils and teachers was endless. Frau Biedermann had in her authoritarian way trodden on too many people's toes. Of course they were all now **laughing up their sleeves** at her unmasking. Our strict headmistress of all people, breaking her own rules.

"I thought you could have knocked me down with a feather when I saw the photo," said van Gogh, grinning with schadenfreude.

Wolfie just kept going around school with a red face. For him, who'd always been so correct and morally **flawless**, the whole thing must have been mega-embarrassing. But I did feel a bit sorry for him. It could be quite violent if Cupid's arrow hit someone of his age. That could well cause you to lose your senses a bit.

"It's not on. This has wide **repercussions**," said Dad at supper time. "I've mobilised the PTA. There's an ex-

---

to summon – herzitieren; issue – *hier:* Ausgabe;
to laugh up one's sleeve – sich ins Fäustchen lachen;
flawless – makellos; repercussions – Nachspiel

traordinary meeting this evening which the school governors are coming to."

"Will you support us?" I asked.

Dad looked at me in astonishment. "Of course I will, what do you think! You've done what was in your power to do, and you've done it fantastically well. Now it's our turn."

I beamed at Mum. "Are you going?"

She nodded.

"Then don't forget to make sure that we don't get a school uniform!" Joker reminded her of his most pressing concern.

It was late, very late, when my parents returned that evening.

All the same, I waited for them in the hall. "So? What did they decide?"

Both of them had to grin. "You'll find out at school tomorrow!"

Meanies!

During the lunch break next day there was in fact yet another school assembly, this time **decreed** from on high. Well, we really were intrigued to see how Frau Biedermann would extract herself from the affair – in the truest sense of the word.

However, Frau Biedermann didn't come. Instead, a

---

meanie – Fiesling;
to decree – anordnen

grey-haired school governor walked, **stooping** rather, to the lectern. Expectant silence.

He cleared his throat and then took the microphone.

"Well, girls and boys, you have proved that you are capable of quite astonishing achievements if it's a question of defending your interests and rights. This revue at the summer party was an excellent communal achievement and symbolises the productive spirit that prevails in our school."

Great!

"The local press reaction," he cleared his throat again, "has brought it to our attention, however, that Frau Biedermann has gone rather too far and has possibly misjudged the significance of democratic freedoms and social contact, indeed of friendship, care and love, for the working climate and school life overall."

Hear, hear!

"The PTA believe, and the governors share their opinion, that scholastic commitment and achievement on the part of the pupils are more readily brought about if they are **fostered** in a climate of freedom, personal responsibility and social **involvement**. The authoritarian measures of Frau Biedermann thus correspond neither to the most recent pedagogical research nor to the spirit of our age nor to our school. The governors have therefore decided, following the urgent requests of the PTA, to relieve Frau Biedermann of her headship.

---

to stoop – gebeugt gehen;
to foster – fördern;
involvement – Einbindung

Moreover, the liaison teachers will, together with the year representatives and student heads, immediately **revise** Frau Biedermann's catalogue of measures and will check that it meets all relevant criteria for social interaction."

Renewed throat-clearing and whispering among the audience.

"What's that supposed to mean? Relevant criteria for social interaction?" asked Greetje.

Before I could explain it to her, Bastian went to the lectern as student head. He shook hands with the governor and thanked him in the name of all the pupils for taking action so quickly. Then he stepped up to the microphone and said, "For everyone who's not quite understood it: we can kiss again in future!"

And before the thunderous cheering drowned out everything else in the hall, he added with an ironic look at Wolfie, "I think that **applies to** students *and* teachers."

Then the hall went wild. Fabian and the Gorillas plunged into the tumult and shortly afterwards I saw Gracia running off, screaming.

"Get your hands off me, don't touch me, you monster!!!" she was yelling at Fabian.

Yes, yes, Beauty and the Beast! I was pretty sure that it would end with a box on the ears, whereby the old order would be restored.

---

to revise – überprüfen;
to apply to – gelten für

Joker hugged me happily. "No short trousers!" he cheered.

Then I, too, was gripped by the general **frenzy**.

Uschi had sat at the piano and the people from the kissing club spontaneously jumped up on the stage and improvised once more the funniest scenes from the revue, and finally the whole hall sang along: *Nobody who'd seen what's gone on here would have believed it: kissing is allowed again!*

I was watching with fascination how all kinds of couples fell into one another's arms, including Franzi and Raffi and Mona and Bastian when Meik pulled me behind the stage.

"I love you," he whispered tenderly into my left ear.

"Really, just me?"

He looked at me with his faithful blue eyes. "Just you! You and only you! I've always loved only you."

"And what about my father and politics?"

"Oh no, Kiki! Change the record!"

He seemed to be genuinely distraught.

I grinned in a **conciliatory** way. "It's fine, it's fine – if everyone's being so ready to compromise today, Kiki can't be left behind. Do what you like, I shan't interfere any more. Maybe I'll even deliver a few leaflets for my father with you. Okay?"

"**That'll do me**," said Meik, "but you'll always take first place, you can trust me on that score."

---

frenzy – Taumel; conciliatory – versöhnlich;
That'll do me. – Das passt.

There you are! Why not at the start? Right from the start, that was all I ever wanted to hear from him.

When we kissed, we overran the film-kiss time again many times over, and my head **buzzed** with: *Your kisses belong only to me …*

Heavens, was I ever happy!

---

to buzz – summen

Mehr über Kiki bei Thienemann:

Schulhof-Flirt & Laufstegträume
Knutschverbot & Herzensdiebe
Liebesfrust & Popstar-Kuss
Jungs & andere Katastrophen
Schoolyard Flirt & Catwalk Dreams

Falls du Lust hast, Bianka Minte-König eine Mail zu schicken, hier die Adresse:
autorin@biankaminte-koenig.de

Minte-König, Bianka:
Kissing Ban & Stolen Hearts
Aus dem Deutschen von Helena Ragg-Kirkby
ISBN 978 3 522 17975 1

Einbandgestaltung und -typographie: Birgit Schössow
Innentypographie: Marlis Killermann
Schrift: Aldus roman und Handwriting Plain
Satz: KCS GmbH, Buchholz/Hamburg
Reproduktion: Medienfabrik, Möglingen
Druck und Bindung: Friedrich Pustet, Regensburg

5 4 3 2 1° 07 08 09 10

www.thienemann.de
www.frechemaedchen.de
www.biankaminte-koenig.de

Freche Mädchen – freche Bücher!

von Bianka Minte-König

Hanna, Mila und Kati im Liebesstress

❑ **Liebestrank & Schokokuss**
208 Seiten · ISBN 978 3 522 17616 3
Wer ist Katis heimlicher Verehrer?

❑ **Superstars & Liebesstress**
208 Seiten · ISBN 978 3 522 17636 1
Sing mir dein schönstes Liebeslied!

❑ **Liebestest & Musenkuss**
192 Seiten · ISBN 978 3 522 17676 7
Ein Freund für Mila muss her!

❑ **Liebeslied & Schulfestküsse**
192 Seiten · ISBN 978 3 522 17759 7
Ist Markus etwa untreu?

❑ **SMS & Liebesstress**
192 Seiten · ISBN 978 3 522 17825 9
Das Liebeskarussell dreht sich weiter

Freche Mädchen – freches Englisch!

❑ **Mobile Phone Love**
208 Seiten · ISBN 978 3 522 17687 3
Hanna is receiving calls and messages from a secret admirer

❑ **Schoolyard Flirt & Catwalk Dreams**
224 Seiten · ISBN 978 3 522 17806 8
Kiki applies to be a model in a fashion show ...

❑ **Summer, Sun & Holiday Love**
336 Seiten · ISBN 978 3 522 17775 7
Seven times flirting in English

Anthologien

❑ **Sommer, Sonne, Ferienliebe**
320 Seiten · ISBN 978 3 522 17686 6
Die sieben schönsten Ferienflirts!

❑ **Liebe, Kuss, O Tannenbaum**
336 Seiten · ISBN 978 3 522 17735 1
Siebenmal Weihnachten und Liebe satt!

❑ **Sommer, Sonne, erste Liebe**
352 Seiten · ISBN 978 3 522 17802 0
Siebenmal erste Liebe!

❑ **Schneeflöckchen, Kuss & Kerzenschein**
256 Seiten · ISBN 978 3 522 17972 0
Acht Winterkuschelgeschichten – echt romantisch!

❑ **Liebe, Küsse, Herzgeschichten**
160 Seiten · ISBN 978 3 522 17734 4
Die zwölf Siegergeschichten des Schreibwettbewerbs

☑ Hab ich schon! – ♥ Muss ich haben!

THIENEMANN